From Your Lips To God's Ear

By

Dr. Ralph Stowe

From Your Lips to God's Ear
By Dr. Ralph Stowe

Pro-Quality Publications
682 North 144th Avenue
Holland, MI 49424

Visit www.1-800-DrStowe.com or call 1-800-DrStowe for more information about Dr. Ralph Stowe.

ISBN
0-9753358-0-4
9-780975-3358-2
© 2004 Dr. Ralph Stowe
All rights reserved.

ISBN 0-9753358-0-4

5 4 5 0 0

9 780975 335802

Library of Congress Control Number: 2004094194
Library of Congress
Cataloging in Publication Division
101 Independence Ave., SE
Washington, DC 20540-4320

Table of Contents

Dedication and Thanks...v

Acknowledgements...vi

Forward by David Cooper vii

Preface by Pastor Thomas Vanden Heuvel...........................ix

Invitational Comment by Reverend Darwin Reedy................... xii

Should I Read This Book?...1

First Things First 3

    What is 'Prayer' in God's Word? 20

Effective Prayer...22

    Present yourself credibly as His son..............................23

    According to God's Word 23

    Pray Always...26

    Not to get God's Attention 26

    Not to get God to do Something...................................27

    Straight from the Word 29

    As a Believer in Jesus...31

    Open the Windows of Heaven.....................................34

The Rights of Believing 40

    Know the Word 42

    We are Protected 43

    We are Heard 46

    We have Redeemed Power 49

    Foundation of Every Christian Endeavor 53

Kinds of Prayer 58

    Prayer that Changes Things.......................................63

        Prayer of Agreement 63

        Binding and Loosing..65

        Intercessory Prayer 74

        Praying in the Spirit 77

        Petition and Supplication.....................................80

    Thanksgiving and Praise 80

    United or Congregational Prayer.................................84

        Praying for the Pastor..88

    Dedication and Worship..91

    Prayer of Committal 92

7 Steps to a Deeper Prayer Life 99

   Step 1: Conduct of life, to include tithing 102

   Step 2: Base upon the Word of God 102

   Step 3: Apply faith... confessions and action 102

   Step 4: Refuse doubt, fear, and defeat 103

   Step 5: Praise God for the receiving 103

   Step 6: Act as though you have already received 103

   Step 7: Thanksgiving 104

Foundations Review 105

The Beginning 113

Appendix I: Verses with 'pray' 114

Appendix II: Strong's definitions 188

Appendix III: Key Words In Context 199

About the Author 238

Dedication and Thanks

This book is dedicated to my family who has long supported me in my journey through life and in my growth.

To my mother, Anna, who taught me to cherish God's word,

To my daughter, Abigail, who has given me much joy;

To my son, Nathanael, who has show that if you teach a child in the ways of God that when he is older he will not depart there from; and

To my wife, Pamela, who has helped me grow in my relationship with God.

Acknowledgements

A special thanks to all who have guided, directed, and challenged my spiritual growth, which has resulted in this study work. From my father, Shirley, who cautioned me about the power of the words of my mouth, to my Swedish Baptist Sunday school teachers like Mr. Hoyt who took the rowdiness of childhood and directed it to constructive learning, to my high school teachers like Mr. Gornick who taught me the value of knowledge, to college professors like Mr. Harriman who guided my philosophical studies and Dr. Panissi who asked if we really understood because that is where the joy is to be found, to others like Mr. Fox who encouraged me to always study and improve myself, to those like Dr. Frigerio who taught me how to investigate and use the pool of knowledge gathered by others and to view it afresh, to those like Mr. Wolfeil who have lovingly challenged my views, and to those like Mr. Benefield who have helped me hone my understanding of the scriptures. and to those like Monet who know that focus is crucial. Thanks to all who have reviewed this manuscript and made valuable contributions. Thank you to Mrs. Laurie Vanden Heuvel who offered ideas about the title of this book.

Forward by David Cooper

It is such an honor to enthusiastically recommend From Your Lips To God's Ear!

I was excited when Dr. Stowe asked me to review this book. Dr. Stowe and I have known each other since our early career days. I was in sales and breaking into the lecture circuit sharing what I had learned. I had been a door-to-door Bible salesman while in college..... And, now I am very pleased to recommend this work that presents dynamic prayer-skills information so that our genuine communication with God can be consistent with the guide presented in the Bible.

When faced with a seemingly impossible situation, how often have you heard someone say, "I guess there's nothing else I can do except pray?" Why is that? Why is prayer all too often the last resort instead of the first defense? Could it be they don't understand God's view of prayer? His view of His Children? Why prayer is such an integral part of our relationship with God? How to pray? What to pray? When to pray?

From Your Lips To God's Ear encourages you to develop your relationship with God through an active prayer life. Understanding how various kinds of prayer is developed and supported through scriptural references and examples. Praying the word of God is emphasized. It is my sincere belief many, many people who read this book will read it about 3 times initially. Then, send dozens of copies away to expand their own influence for more people to become closer to God through prayer.

Dr. Stowe's depth of knowledge could only have come from years of lengthy study on the subject of prayer and much practice of communing with the Holy Spirit. From my relationship with Dr. Stowe, I can tell you that he lives in the benefits that he has presented here. Just as it has for me, I hope this book earns a revered place in your TOP-10 most frequently recommended books! I can genuinely recommend this book for the newest members of God's family to senior saints still seeking to draw ever closer to God.

David Cooper
Memphis, Tennessee
April 28, 2004
www.DavidCooper.com

Preface by Pastor Thomas Vanden Heuvel

Prayer is the most important part of the Christian life. A very familiar Reformation Catechism puts it this way: "Why is prayer necessary for Christians? Because it is the chief part of thankfulness which God requires of us, and because God will give His grace and Holy Spirit to those only who, with hearty sighing, unceasingly beg them of Him and thank Him for them" (*Heidelberg Catechism*, Q and A 116). "Prayer is the offering up of our desires to God in the name of Christ, by the help of His Spirit, with confession of sins and thankful acknowledgment of His mercies" (*Westminster Larger Catechism*, Q and A 178).

Dr Ralph Stowe has written a very helpful book on this subject. As I read it I was reminded of Job 23:3,4: "Oh that I knew where I might find him! that I might come even to his seat! I would order my cause before him, and fill my mouth with arguments." The word "arguments" does not mean quarrels or disagreements, but grounds to buttress my prayer and my requests to God. We see this in the prayer of Abraham for his nephew

Lot who had "pitched his tent toward Sodom" and was now living in this wicked and corrupt city. God had told Abraham that He was going to destroy the cities of Sodom and Gomorrah because of their wickedness. Abraham prayed in Genesis 18:23-32 saying: "Wilt Thou also destroy the righteous with the wicked?" You recall how Abraham goes from fifty righteous to ten righteous, and as he progresses, he uses this powerful argument: "Shall not the Judge of all the earth do right?" (Genesis 18:25). We may pray to God with confidence using His own Being and works and words as our grounds or arguments buttressing our prayers.

Moses did this on Mt. Sinai when God threatened to destroy the children of Israel for their worshiping of the golden calf, and to begin a new people with Moses. Moses prayed and pleaded with God not to do this, using powerful arguments recorded in Exodus 32:7-14. Moses pleaded on the basis of God's own word of promise to Abraham, Isaac, and Jacob. Moses also used the powerful argument of God's reputation saying: "Wherefore should the Egyptians speak and say: 'For mischief did he bring them in the mountains, and to consume them from the face of the earth?'" (Exodus 32:12). We may come to God with effective prayer as we come using what He has given us in His word.

The Bible has many examples of the prayers of God's people using who God is, what He has promised, and what He has done, to buttress their prayers to Him. Other wonderful examples are David in Psalm 51; Hezekiah in Isaiah 37:14-20; and God's wonderful answer to Hezekiah's prayer in Isaiah 37:21-36.

I hope that this book by Dr. Stowe will help you to pray biblically and effectively. The goal of our lives and of our prayer is to glorify God and enjoy Him forever. May you experience the truth of the statement that "prayer is the chief part of thankfulness" which we can offer to the Lord who made us, who redeemed us in Christ, and who loves us with an undying love.

Rev. Thomas Vanden Heuvel
Covenant Presbyterian Church (PCA)
July 20, 2004

Invitational Comment by Reverend Darwin Reedy

It is a pleasure to invite you to read this book, which is one of vital interest and daily need on both a personal and corporate basis. Dr. Ralph Stowe, known to me as Ralph and Brother, is dedicated to exploring religious thoughts with scriptural support. No matter, where you are in your "personal walk", this will inform, challenge, and expand you.

Dr. Stowe has needed, like all of us, to be "in prayer." Also, we have spent hours in discussion of the various truths, which are revealed through prayer; and as we are all "works in process", it is an ever-evolving process. Also, it is never out of keeping to invite the "Spirit", the "Holy Spirit", the "Source", or whatever power you believe in, to aid, assist, and admonish.

Good reading and exploring.

Rev. Darwin D. Reedy
Pinellas Park, Florida
March 26, 2004

From Your Lips To God's Ear

Should I Read This Book?

Every work is penned with a specific audience in mind. This work is no exception. It is written for believers in Jesus the Christ. Do not despair, if you are not yet in the target audience, the chapter 'First Things First' will provide you with sufficient information to allow you to respond to the call to accept Jesus as your Savior.

Christians have learned prayer in large by trial and error. We watch those around us and emulate them. Some of us simply use the Lord's Prayer as our model and get locked into a rote type of prayer. Yet others have studied the scriptures in great depth, but have not focused upon the techniques which prayer requires.

From Your Lips To God's Ear

What follows is a study of prayer, types of prayer, and reviews the benefits of prayer. We have used the Authorized King James Version for convenience, unless otherwise noted. We anticipate both scholar and novice will find benefit in the pages that follow.

From Your Lips To God's Ear

First Things First

We are set apart by the Father when we believe and accept Jesus the Christ as our Savior, Redeemer, Lord, and Brother. He has made us free from all the power of Satan.

Rom 5:8-19 But God commendeth his love toward us, in that, while we were yet sinners, Christ died for us. Much more then, being now justified by his blood, we shall be saved from wrath through him. For if, when we were enemies, we were reconciled to God by the death of his Son, much more, being reconciled, we shall be saved by his life. And not only so, but we also joy in God through our Lord Jesus Christ, by whom we have now received the atonement. Wherefore, as by one man sin entered into the world, and death by sin; and so death passed upon all men, for that all have sinned: (For until the law sin was in the world: but sin is not imputed when there is no law. Nevertheless death reigned from Adam to Moses, even over

From Your Lips To God's Ear

them that had not sinned after the similitude of Adam's transgression, who is the figure of him that was to come. But not as the offence, so also is the free gift. For if through the offence of one many be dead, much more the grace of God, and the gift by grace, which is by one man, Jesus Christ, hath abounded unto many. And not as it was by one that sinned, so is the gift: for the judgment was by one to condemnation, but the free gift is of many offences unto justification. For if by one man's offence death reigned by one; much more they which receive abundance of grace and of the gift of righteousness shall reign in life by one, Jesus Christ.) Therefore as by the offence of one judgment came upon all men to condemnation; even so by the righteousness of one the free gift came upon all men unto justification of life. For as by one man's disobedience many were made sinners, so by the obedience of one shall many be made righteous.

From Your Lips To God's Ear

Colossians 1:12-22 Giving thanks unto the Father, which hath made us meet to be partakers of the inheritance of the saints in light: Who hath delivered us from the power of darkness, and hath translated us into the kingdom of his dear Son: 14 In whom we have redemption through his blood, even the forgiveness of sins: Who is the image of the invisible God, the firstborn of every creature: For by him were all things created, that are in heaven, and that are in earth, visible and invisible, whether they be thrones, or dominions, or principalities, or powers: all things were created by him, and for him: And he is before all things, and by him all things consist. And he is the head of the body, the church: who is the beginning, the firstborn from the dead; that in all things he might have the preeminence. For it pleased the Father that in him should all fullness dwell; And, having made peace through the blood of his cross, by him to reconcile all things unto himself; by

by Dr. Ralph Stowe

From Your Lips To God's Ear

> *him, I say, whether they be things in earth, or things in heaven. And you, that were sometime alienated and enemies in your mind by wicked works, yet now hath he reconciled In the body of his flesh through death, to present you holy and unblameable and unreproveable in his sight:*

Sixteen scriptures from 12 different books of the Bible state we are the sons of the Living God when we make Jesus the Lord of our life. John 17:22-26; Romans 8:14; 2 Corinthians 6:14; Galatians 3:26; Galatians 4:5; Ephesians 2:1-7; Philippians 2:15; Col 1:12-22; 1 Thessalonians 5:5; Hebrews 2:11-13; I Peter 2:9-10; 2 Peter 1:17-21; I John 3:2; Jude 4; Revelation 1:4-6; Revelation 3:21 all tell us that we are the sons of God. There are only two families in the earth: Those who have made Jesus Lord of their lives, and those who have not.

We are delivered from darkness and our identification is with the all powerful God and His Son, our brother. Every thought, word, and action gives allegiance to one or the other of the two families. We need to be careful to identify with the Righteousness of the Lord of

From Your Lips To God's Ear
Life.

> *John 10:10 The thief cometh not, but for to steal, and to kill, and to destroy: I am come that they might have life, and that they might have it more abundantly.*

> *I John 3:8 He that committeth sin is of the devil; for the devil sinneth from the beginning. For this purpose the Son of God was manifested, that he might destroy the works of the devil.*

> *I John 3:9-10 Whosoever is born of God doth not commit sin; for his seed remaineth in him: and he cannot sin, because he is born of God. 10 In this the children of God are manifest, and the children of the devil: whosoever doeth not righteousness is not of God, neither he that loveth not his brother.*

So, are you identifying with the fallen Adam in sin or with the resurrected righteousness through Jesus? Who is the High Priest over your house? We answer with our thoughts, our words, our actions, for out of the abundance of

From Your Lips To God's Ear

the heart flow the issues of life.

John 17:1-26 These words spake Jesus, and lifted up his eyes to heaven, and said, Father, the hour is come; glorify thy Son, that thy Son also may glorify thee: As thou hast given him power over all flesh, that he should give eternal life to as many as thou hast given him. And this is life eternal, that they might know thee the only true God, and Jesus Christ, whom thou hast sent. I have glorified thee on the earth: I have finished the work which thou gavest me to do. And now, O Father, glorify thou me with thine own self with the glory which I had with thee before the world was. I have manifested thy name unto the men which thou gavest me out of the world: thine they were, and thou gavest them me; and they have kept thy word. Now they have known that all things whatsoever thou hast given me are of thee. For I have given unto them the words which thou gavest me; and they have received them, and have known surely that I came out from thee,

From Your Lips To God's Ear

and they have believed that thou didst send me. I pray for them: I pray not for the world, but for them which thou hast given me; for they are thine. And all mine are thine, and thine are mine; and I am glorified in them. And now I am no more in the world, but these are in the world, and I come to thee. Holy Father, keep through thine own name those whom thou hast given me, that they may be one, as we are. While I was with them in the world, I kept them in thy name: those that thou gavest me I have kept, and none of them is lost, but the son of perdition; that the scripture might be fulfilled. And now come I to thee; and these things I speak in the world, that they might have my joy fulfilled in themselves. I have given them thy word; and the world hath hated them, because they are not of the world, even as I am not of the world. I pray not that thou shouldest take them out of the world, but that thou shouldest keep them from the evil. They are not of the world, even as I am not of the

From Your Lips To God's Ear

world. Sanctify them through thy truth: thy word is truth. As thou hast sent me into the world, even so have I also sent them into the world.

And for their sakes I sanctify myself, that they also might be sanctified through the truth. Neither pray I for these alone, but for them also which shall believe on me through their word; That they all may be one; as thou, Father, art in me, and I in thee, that they also may be one in us: that the world may believe that thou hast sent me. And the glory which thou gavest me I have given them; that they may be one, even as we are one: I in them, and thou in me, that they may be made perfect in one; and that the world may know that thou hast sent me, and hast loved them, as thou hast loved me. Father, I will that they also, whom thou hast given me, be with me where I am; that they may behold my glory, which thou hast given me: for thou lovedst me before the foundation of the world. O righteous Father, the world hath not known thee: but I have known

by Dr. Ralph Stowe

From Your Lips To God's Ear

thee, and these have known that thou hast sent me. And I have declared unto them thy name, and will declare it: that the love wherewith thou hast loved me may be in them, and I in them.

Heb 4:16 Let us therefore come boldly unto the throne of grace, that we may obtain mercy, and find grace to help in time of need.

We are now set free from any evil power if we invoke God's power, given us by Jesus, over the lord of the fallen Adam... yes over Satan.

Eph 2:1-22 And you hath he quickened, who were dead in trespasses and sins; Wherein in time past ye walked according to the course of this world, according to the prince of the power of the air, the spirit that now worketh in the children of disobedience: Among whom also we all had our conversation in times past in the lusts of our flesh, fulfilling the desires of the flesh and of the mind; and were by nature the children of

From Your Lips To God's Ear

wrath, even as others. But God, who is rich in mercy, for his great love wherewith he loved us, Even when we were dead in sins, hath quickened us together with Christ, (by grace ye are saved;) And hath raised us up together, and made us sit together in heavenly places in Christ Jesus: That in the ages to come he might shew the exceeding riches of his grace in his kindness toward us through Christ Jesus. For by grace are ye saved through faith; and that not of yourselves: it is the gift of God: Not of works, lest any man should boast. For we are his workmanship, created in Christ Jesus unto good works, which God hath before ordained that we should walk in them. Wherefore remember, that ye being in time past Gentiles in the flesh, who are called Uncircumcision by that which is called the Circumcision in the flesh made by hands; That at that time ye were without Christ, being aliens from the commonwealth of Israel, and strangers from the covenants of promise, having no hope, and

From Your Lips To God's Ear

without God in the world: But now in Christ Jesus ye who sometimes were far off are made nigh by the blood of Christ. For he is our peace, who hath made both one, and hath broken down the middle wall of partition between us; Having abolished in his flesh the enmity, even the law of commandments contained in ordinances; for to make in himself of twain one new man, so making peace; And that he might reconcile both unto God in one body by the cross, having slain the enmity thereby: And came and preached peace to you which were afar off, and to them that were nigh. For through him we both have access by one Spirit unto the Father. Now therefore ye are no more strangers and foreigners, but fellow citizens with the saints, and of the household of God; And are built upon the foundation of the apostles and prophets, Jesus Christ himself being the chief corner stone; In whom all the building fitly framed together groweth unto an holy temple in the Lord: In whom ye also

From Your Lips To God's Ear

> *are builded together for an habitation of God through the Spirit.*

So Jesus died that we can be alive. We are restored to the authority that God gave to Adam. Jesus gave us the power over Satan. He then translated us from the Kingdom of Darkness into the Kingdom of Life. Jesus took our debt in order to give us life. He gave His life to give us redemption. He took our sins to give us His righteousness. He took our sickness and disease to give us His divine life. If you have not taken Jesus as your savior, you need to do it now. You might pray a prayer of salvation as outlined:

> "Dear Heavenly Father, I come to You in the Name of Jesus. Your Word says, in John 6:37 "... him that cometh to me I will in no wise cast out...'. In Romans 10:13 You said 'Whosoever shall call upon the name of the Lord shall be saved'. I am calling on Your Name, so I know You have saved me now! I believe in my heart that Jesus Christ is the Son of God. I believe that He paid the price for my sins when He died on the cross and was raised from the dead for my justification. I confess Him now as my Lord as you said in Romans 10:9-10 '... if thou shalt confess with thy mouth the Lord Jesus,

From Your Lips To God's Ear

and shalt believe in thine heart that God hath raised him from the dead, thou shalt be saved. For with the heart man believeth unto righteousness; and with the mouth, confession is made unto salvation...'. I have now become the righteousness of God in Christ according to 2 Corinthians 5:21 and I am saved! Thank you Lord!!"

Look at it from Lucifer's eyes [Satan's eyes], wanting to be in charge of all the earth, knowing how beautiful he was and the position he held in heaven. When iniquity was found in him, he was cast down! He had no authority over anything. God created man in His own image. What rage Satan must have experienced! Adam had all authority over everything in the garden. Satan set about cheating Adam out of his inheritance by deceiving Adam's wife. Adam bowed his knee to Satan and did as he asked. Immediately God put Satan on notice of a coming redemption. Satan then had to attempt to subdue every child that would be born so he would not miss destroying the coming redeemer. Having missed the redeemer, he now fights to keep us from understanding what Jesus has done for us. Unfortunately, many well-intended 'Religious Christians' have fallen into a misunderstanding and are helping Satan limit

From Your Lips To God's Ear

the power of the sons of God.

> *Romans16:25-26 Now to him that is of power to stablish you according to my gospel, and the preaching of Jesus Christ, according to the revelation of the mystery, which was kept secret since the world began, But now is made manifest, and by the scriptures of the prophets, according to the commandment of the everlasting God, made known to all nations for the obedience of faith:*

> *Isaiah 52:14-15 As many were astonied at thee; his visage was so marred more than any man, and his form more than the sons of men: So shall he sprinkle many nations; the kings shall shut their mouths at him: for that which had not been told them shall they see; and that which they had not heard shall they consider.*

> *Acts 2:31-33 He seeing this before spake of the resurrection of Christ, that his soul was not left in hell, neither his flesh did see corruption.*

From Your Lips To God's Ear

This Jesus hath God raised up, whereof we all are witnesses. Therefore being by the right hand of God exalted, and having received of the Father the promise of the Holy Ghost, he hath shed forth this, which ye now see and hear.

Acts 2:27 Because thou wilt not leave my soul in hell, neither wilt thou suffer thine Holy One to see corruption.

Acts 2:22-24 Ye men of Israel, hear these words; Jesus of Nazareth, a man approved of God among you by miracles and wonders and signs, which God did by him in the midst of you, as ye yourselves also know: Him, being delivered by the determinate counsel and foreknowledge of God, ye have taken, and by wicked hands have crucified and slain: Whom God hath raised up, having loosed the pains of death: because it was not possible that he should be holden of it.

From Your Lips To God's Ear

Rom 3:19-26 Now we know that what things soever the law saith, it saith to them who are under the law: that every mouth may be stopped, and all the world may become guilty before God. Therefore by the deeds of the law there shall no flesh be justified in his sight: for by the law is the knowledge of sin. But now the righteousness of God without the law is manifested, being witnessed by the law and the prophets; Even the righteousness of God which is by faith of Jesus Christ unto all and upon all them that believe: for there is no difference: For all have sinned, and come short of the glory of God; Being justified freely by his grace through the redemption that is in Christ Jesus: Whom God hath set forth to be a propitiation through faith in his blood, to declare his righteousness for the remission of sins that are past, through the forbearance of God; To declare, I say, at this time his righteousness: that he might be just, and the justifier of him which believeth in Jesus.

by Dr. Ralph Stowe   18

From Your Lips To God's Ear

2 Cor 5:17-19 Therefore if any man be in Christ, he is a new creature: old things are passed away; behold, all things are become new. And all things are of God, who hath reconciled us to himself by Jesus Christ, and hath given to us the ministry of reconciliation; To wit, that God was in Christ, reconciling the world unto himself, not imputing their trespasses unto them; and hath committed unto us the word of reconciliation.

2 Corinthians 6:14-16 Be ye not unequally yoked together with unbelievers: for what fellowship hath righteousness with unrighteousness? and what communion hath light with darkness? And what concord hath Christ with Belial? or what part hath he that believeth with an infidel? And what agreement hath the temple of God with idols? for ye are the temple of the living God; as God hath said, I will dwell in them, and walk in them; and I will be their

by Dr. Ralph Stowe

From Your Lips To God's Ear

God, and they shall be my people.

2 Corinthians 6:18 And will be a Father unto you, and ye shall be my sons and daughters, saith the Lord Almighty.

What is 'Prayer' in God's Word?

If we are going to pray to God, it would be wise for us to know what that really means. Tradition may or may not have it right. Let's do a little detective work to find out!

We turn to the scholarly work of Strong. His concordance shows each and every time the word pray, prayed, praying, or prayer is used in the Authorized King James version (actually Strong has listed all words each and every time they are used!) and then gives the definition of the actual word used in the manuscript.

If you are really into this sort of thing, please see Appendix I for the list, and Appendix II for the Strong's definitions used for these words.

For the rest of us, suffice it to say that prayer is a *verbal* communication or petition. We can praise God

From Your Lips To God's Ear
or say His words back to Him in a petition.

From Your Lips To God's Ear

Effective **Prayer**

1 Timothy 2:1-4 I exhort therefore, that, first of all, supplications, prayers, intercessions, and giving of thanks be made for all men; For kings, and for all that are in authority; that we may lead a quiet and peaceable life in all godliness and honesty. For this is good and acceptable in the sight of God our Savior; Who will have all men to be saved, and to come unto the knowledge of the truth.

> *James 1:22 But be ye doers of the word, and not hearers only, deceiving your own selves.*

There are ideas about prayer that are not scriptural. God built safeguards into the prayer system, not to keep us out but to keep Satan from taking advantage of us.

For example, a bank has your money but it has safeguards so that others cannot get your money. There are specific steps you must take to get your money. They will not just give it to you because you say you have money with them and you want something. You must properly complete a withdrawal form. You must remind

From Your Lips To God's Ear

them of your account number. You must show proof or have a witness that you are who you say. Similarly, if you do not ask the bank for your money, they do not call you on the phone and ask if you might have a need!

Present yourself credibly as His son

By not following God's Word we can hinder our prayers.

> *1 Peter 3:7 Likewise, ye husbands, dwell with them according to knowledge, giving honour unto the wife, as unto the weaker vessel, and as being heirs together of the grace of life; that your prayers be not hindered.*

According to God's Word

We do not have because we do not ask or we ask amiss. We have to ask correctly.

> *James 4:2 Ye lust, and have not: ye kill, and desire to have, and cannot obtain: ye fight and war, yet ye have not, because ye ask not. Ye ask, and receive not, because ye ask*

From Your Lips To God's Ear

> *amiss, that ye may consume it upon your lust.*

Realize God has interest in our well-being! We do not have to beg God. It is His will for us to be healthy, and it is His nature to heal.... Shalom! We must apply the Word of God. God's word is the last Word, not the word of any others. Fight for what is yours despite what others may say.... Our weapons are not carnal. Fear and guilt are enemies of the Word of God.

God's word is sure.

> *Ps 119:87-89   They had almost consumed me upon earth; but I forsook not thy precepts. Quicken me after thy lovingkindness; so shall I keep the testimony of thy mouth. For ever, O LORD, thy word is settled in heaven.*

> *James 4:7-8   Submit yourselves therefore to God. Resist the devil, and he will flee from you. Draw nigh to God, and he will draw nigh to you.   Cleanse your hands, ye sinners; and purify your hearts, ye double minded.*

From Your Lips To God's Ear

> *Luke 18:1 And he spoke a parable unto them to this end, that men ought always to pray, and not faint.*

Prayer is always available, not just to the goodie goodie. He hears your prayer because you are His child. There is no situation, which would disqualify you from prayer. The deepest of sinners in the deepest of sin can still pray the prayer of repentance. From that point, he qualifies to continue into the other fields of prayer because Jesus is our faithful High Priest. The only situation from which there is no deliverance is the rebellious refusal to pray at all. God's Word is His part of our prayer life. His part is available to whomsoever will: His mighty Word is offered to whom so ever will. Your entire life ought to be centered on prayer!

> *Acts 2:21 And it shall come to pass, that whosoever shall call on the name of the Lord shall be saved.*

> *Acts 10:34 Then Peter opened his mouth, and said, of a truth I perceive that God is no respecter of persons: 35 But in every nation he that feareth Him, and worketh righteousness, is accepted with Him.*

by Dr. Ralph Stowe

From Your Lips To God's Ear

Pray Always

Your life ought to be centered on prayer! God wants us to rely upon Him for our every need and to focus on the fact that He is the supplier of all good things. We are then free of our circumstances and we receive what God has already given us. The only situation that is hopeless is the one we choose not to pray about and receive God's resolve.

> *Luke 18:1 And he spoke a parable unto them to this end, that men ought always to pray, and not faint. My God will hear me when I pray in Jesus name! And He will do the same for you, if you are saved.*

Not to get God's Attention

Prayer is not trying to get God's attention.

> *Hebrews 4:12-16   For the word of God is quick, and powerful, and sharper than any two edged sword, piercing even to the dividing asunder of soul and spirit, and of the joints and marrow, and is a*

From Your Lips To God's Ear

discerner of the thoughts and intents of the heart. Neither is there any creature that is not manifest in His sight: but all things are naked and opened unto the eyes of Him with whom we have to do. Seeing then that we have a great High Priest, that is passed into the heavens, Jesus the Son of God, let us hold fast our profession. For we have not an High Priest which cannot be touched with the feeling of our infirmities: but was in all points tempted like as we are, yet without sin. Let us therefore come boldly unto the throne of grace, that we may obtain mercy, and find grace to help in time of need.

Not to get God to do Something

Prayer is not trying to get God to do something. Prayer is communication with God receiving what He has already given us in Christ Jesus. Pray in the name of Jesus what God has said and we shall receive!

"Father, in Jesus name, I pray to you that I might be set free in my Spirit life, my Soul,

From Your Lips To God's Ear

> my Body, my Financial life, my Social life. Thank you in the name of your Son Jesus the Anointed One."

So by being obedient, we place ourselves in a position where God is free to bless us and we can receive what we ask! Go to the scriptures and find the verses that state the blessing you want and include that in your prayer. God is true to His Word and is bound by it. So our struggle is not with God, God is the answer to the problem.

> *Num 23:19-20 God is not a man, that he should lie; neither the son of man, that he should repent: hath he said, and shall he not do it? or hath he spoken, and shall he not make it good? Behold, I have received commandment to bless: and he hath blessed; and I cannot reverse it.*

> *Matthew 21:21-22 Jesus answered and said unto them, Verily I say unto you If ye have faith, and doubt not, ye shall not only do this which is done to the fig tree, but also if ye shall say unto this mountain, Be thou removed, and be thou cast into the sea; it shall be done. And all*

From Your Lips To God's Ear

> *things, whatsoever ye shall ask in prayer, believing, ye shall receive.*
>
> *Mark 11:24 Therefore I say unto you, What things soever ye desire, when ye pray, believe that ye receive them, and ye shall have them.*
>
> *Isaiah 59:1 Behold, the Lord's hand is not shortened, that it cannot save; neither His ear heavy, that it cannot hear:*
>
> *Luke 18:1 And he spake a parable unto them to this end, that men ought always to pray, and not to faint;*

Straight from the Word

Study of God's Word, the Bible, is fundamental. If we do not know what the Word has in it, we cannot hope to know what is available to us, and we will fall prey to silly traditions. Now, knowing what the Word says, I can have faith. If I have faith I believe the word of God, If I have faith I act upon the word of God, If I have faith I

by Dr. Ralph Stowe   29

From Your Lips To God's Ear

receive the word of God in my life. To not receive God's gifts is rejecting God, or showing Satan that we do not really believe the Word. We have the right to believe and an obligation to receive!

> *Luke 13:10-11 And he was teaching in one of the synagogues on the sabbath. And, behold, there was a woman which had a spirit of infirmity eighteen years, and was bowed together, and could in no wise lift up herself.*

Jesus knew that benefits are always appropriate to receive.

> *Luke 13:16 And ought not this woman, being a daughter of Abraham, whom Satan hath bound, lo, these eighteen years, be loosed from this bond on the sabbath day?*

> *Galatians 3:13-14 Christ hath redeemed us from the curse of the law, being made a curse for us: for it is written, Cursed is everyone that hangeth on a tree: That the blessing of Abraham might come on the Gentiles, through Jesus Christ; that we might receive the promise of the Spirit through faith.*

From Your Lips To God's Ear

> *Galatians 3:28-29 There is neither Jew nor Greek, there is neither bond nor free, there is neither male nor female: for ye are all one in Christ Jesus. And if ye be Christ's, then are ye Abraham's seed, and heirs according to the promise.*

As a Believer in Jesus

As believers in Jesus and His Anointing, we have a right to believe and receive. At Jesus' crucifixion we inherited the blessings and we were redeemed from the curses. Therefore, we have it all now. We have all that Jesus had and what he purchased.

> *Romans 4:16-25 Therefore it is of faith, that it might be by grace; to the end the promise might be sure to all the seed; not to that only which is of the law, but to that also which is of the faith of Abraham; who is the father of us all, (As it is written, I have made thee a father of many nations,) before Him whom he believed, even God, who*

From Your Lips To God's Ear

quickeneth the dead, and calleth those things which be not as though they were. Who against hope believed in hope, that he might become the father of many nations, according to that which was spoken, So shall thy seed be. And being not weak in faith, he considered not his own body now dead, when he was about an hundred years old, neither, yet the deadness of Sarah's womb: He staggered not at the promise of God through unbelief; but was strong in faith, giving glory to God; And being fully persuaded that, what he had promised, he was able also to perform. And therefore it was imputed to him for righteousness. Now it was not written for his sake alone, that it was imputed to him; But for us also, to whom it shall be imputed, if we believe on Him that raised up Jesus our Lord from the dead; Who was delivered for our offences, and was raised again for our justification.

Galatians 3:14 That the blessing of Abraham might come on the

From Your Lips To God's Ear

> *Gentiles, through Jesus Christ; that we might receive the promise of the Spirit through faith.*
>
> *Galatians 3:29   And if ye be Christ's, then are ye Abraham's seed, and heirs according to the promise.*

We pray over our food, for example. We need to know what the Word says about how we should pray. Do we ask God to bless the missionaries or add to our finances when we are praying over the food? I would think not! We need to look into the Word and remember that God has promised to give good pleasure to our mouth and to bless what we take so that nothing harms us and that sickness and disease would be taken away from our midst. We might pray something like this then,

> "Father, we come to you in Jesus name, we thank you for this food that you have blessed us with and which we are about to receive. We know these come from you because your Word tells us in Psalm 23 that 'Thou preparest a table before me'; We thank you for the nourishment to our bodies as it says in 1 Timothy 4: 5 'the meat we are about to eat has been sanctified by the Word of God and by prayer'; We thank you

From Your Lips To God's Ear

for the refreshment we are about to drink because we know from Mark 16:17 '...if [we] drink any deadly thing, it shall not hurt [us]'; We praise Your Holy Name that we are protected from any diseased food for You said in Psalms 91:10 'There shall no evil befall thee, neither shall any plague come nigh thy dwelling'; and we thank you for the good taste of the food we are about to eat, for You say in Psalms 103 'Who satisfieth thy mouth with good things; so that thy youth is renewed like the eagle's.' We thank you and say these things because You have said to us in Isaiah 43: 26 'Put me in remembrance: let us plead together: declare thou, that thou mayest be justified'.

Thank you in the name of your Son Jesus the Anointed One."

Open the Windows of Heaven

I once heard it said that the best thing we could do for the poor is not to be one of them. If you review the heroes of the Bible, you will find that each and every one of them had enough to share with others. The sharing came in many forms, but always with purpose and joy. So how can we be in that position? Of course, we and

From Your Lips To God's Ear

we alone can choose our attitude of joy. What about the abundance to share? How can we pray for our finances and be consistent with the Word of God?

> *II Corinthians 9:6-8 But this I say, He which soweth sparingly shall reap also sparingly: and he which soweth bountifully shall reap also bountifully. Every man according as he purposeth in his heart, so let him give; not grudgingly, or of necessity: for God loveth a cheerful giver. And God is able to make all grace abound toward you; that ye always having all sufficiency in all things, may abound to every good work:*

God is abounding toward me, so I should abound toward Him. God meets my needs by my giving when I give joyfully and freely. Giving is not to get, not to be noticed, not to get credit, but to be obedient. How can we give if we are poor? How can we be like Jesus if we are poor?

Jesus was rich. His earthly father was a skilled tradesman in business for himself. He was taxed and inquired at every hotel available to check in when Mary was about to give birth. No rooms were available, so Joseph had to accept a room in the stable! Not because he was poor,

From Your Lips To God's Ear

but because of the crowd in Jerusalem.

> *Luke 2:7 And she brought forth her firstborn son, and wrapped him in swaddling clothes, and laid him in a manger; because there was no room for them in the inn.*

Jesus was presented with gifts of frankincense, gold, and myrrh. Jesus' father, Joseph, was financially able to go down to Egypt to protect his son.

> *Matt 2:11-15 And when they were come into the house, they saw the young child with Mary his mother, and fell down, and worshipped him: and when they had opened their treasures, they presented unto him gifts; gold, and frankincense, and myrrh. And being warned of God in a dream that they should not return to Herod, they departed into their own country another way. And when they were departed, behold, the angel of the Lord appeareth to Joseph in a dream, saying, Arise, and take the young child and his mother, and flee into Egypt, and be thou there until I bring thee word: for Herod will seek the young child to destroy him. When he arose, he*

From Your Lips To God's Ear

> *took the young child and his mother by night, and departed into Egypt: And was there until the death of Herod: that it might be fulfilled which was spoken of the Lord by the prophet, saying, Out of Egypt have I called my son.*

Joseph was rich enough to go to worship to Jerusalem every year.

> *Luke 2:41-42 Now his parents went to Jerusalem every year at the feast of the passover. And when he was twelve years old, they went up to Jerusalem after the custom of the feast.*

Jesus' ministry was so rich they had to have a treasurer. The ministry had so much money; no one even noticed that the treasurer, Judas, was stealing.

> *John 12:3-6 Then took Mary a pound of ointment of spikenard, very costly, and anointed the feet of Jesus, and wiped his feet with her hair: and the house was filled with the odour of the ointment. Then saith one of his disciples, Judas Iscariot, Simon's son, which should betray him, Why was not this ointment sold for three hundred*

From Your Lips To God's Ear

> *pence, and given to the poor? This he said, not that he cared for the poor; but because he was a thief, and had the bag, and bare what was put therein.*

The ministry had so much money that it could have feed the 5,000 had there been a store nearby.

> *Luke 9:12-14 And when the day began to wear away, then came the twelve, and said unto him, Send the multitude away, that they may go into the towns and country round about, and lodge, and get victuals: for we are here in a desert place. But he said unto them, Give ye them to eat. And they said, We have no more but five loaves and two fishes; except we should go and buy meat for all this people. For they were about five thousand men. And he said to his disciples, Make them sit down by fifties in a company.*

At Jesus death, he was wearing such an expensive coat that the guards did not want to rip it apart to divide as they usually did.

> *John 19:23-24 Then the soldiers, when they had crucified Jesus, took his garments, and made four parts,*

From Your Lips To God's Ear

to every soldier a part; and also his coat: now the coat was without seam, woven from the top throughout. They said therefore among themselves, Let us not rend it, but cast lots for it, whose it shall be: that the scripture might be fulfilled, which saith, They parted my raiment among them, and for my vesture they did cast lots. These things therefore the soldiers did.

So, if we are to be like Jesus or any of the other heroes of the Bible, we must be wise with our money and have abundance to be able to bless others.

From Your Lips To God's Ear

The Rights of Believing

Prayer is not trying to get something from God.

Hebrews 4:12-16 For the word of God is quick, and powerful, and sharper than any two-edged sword, piercing even to the dividing asunder of soul and spirit, and of the joints and marrow, and is a discerner of the thoughts and intents of the heart. Neither is there any creature that is not manifest in his sight: but all things are naked and opened unto the eyes of him with whom we have to do. Seeing then that we have a great high priest that is passed into the heavens, Jesus the Son of God, let us hold fast our profession. For we have not an high priest which cannot be touched with the feeling of our infirmities; but was in all points tempted like as we are, yet without sin. Let us therefore come boldly unto the throne of grace, that we may obtain mercy, and find grace to help in time of need.

by Dr. Ralph Stowe

From Your Lips To God's Ear

Our prayers are not answered based upon our fasting, nor based upon our acting good, nor upon our giving generously. No. Not because we have earned the right. We have the right to ask and receive because God's Word says we have the right. We, as believers in Christ, just simply need to believe in the Word.

> *Matthew 21:21-22 Jesus answered and said unto them, Verily I say unto you, If ye have faith, and doubt not, ye shall not only do this which is done to the fig tree, but also if ye shall say unto this mountain, Be thou removed, and be thou cast into the sea; it shall be done. And all things, whatsoever ye shall ask in prayer, believing, ye shall receive.*

> *Mark 11:24-25 Therefore I say unto you, What things soever ye desire, when ye pray, believe that ye receive them, and ye shall have them. And when ye stand praying, forgive, if ye have ought against any: that your Father also which is in heaven may forgive you your trespasses.*

by Dr. Ralph Stowe

From Your Lips To God's Ear

Know the Word

We must stay in the Word to be able to know what it says. We need to read the Word and we need to hear the Word. We need to listen to sermons, discuss the Word with friends, study the Word, or whatever we can to be able to fully understand what God wants for us and wants to give us.

> *Mark 4:22-25 For there is nothing hid, which shall not be manifested; neither was any thing kept secret, but that it should come abroad. If any man have ears to hear, let him hear. And he said unto them, Take heed what ye hear: with what measure ye mete, it shall be measured to you: and unto you that hear shall more be given. For he that hath, to him shall be given: and he that hath not, from him shall be taken even that which he hath.*

> *James 4:2-3 Ye lust, and have not: ye kill, and desire to have, and cannot obtain: ye fight and war, yet ye have not, because ye ask not. Ye ask, and receive not, because ye ask*

From Your Lips To God's Ear

> *amiss, that ye may consume it upon your lusts.*

We are Protected

Should anyone move against us, God will protect us and fight our battles if we ask Him. We are to pray for our enemies, but God has told us that nothing will harm us. How can we do that? How can we pray to be protected from our enemies and at the same time pray for them? Well, let us look at some scriptures.

> *Isaiah 54:10 For the mountains shall depart, and the hills be removed; but my kindness shall not depart from thee, neither shall the covenant of my peace be removed, saith the LORD that hath mercy on thee.*

> *Isaiah 54:17 No weapon that is formed against thee shall prosper; and every tongue that shall rise against thee in judgment thou shall condemn. This is the heritage of the servants of the Lord, and their righteousness is of me, saith the Lord.*

From Your Lips To God's Ear

Let us consider a possible prayer to sound something like:

> "Father, in Jesus name, we ask you to bless Bill and we thank you for your infinite mercy, for your kindness. But we also remind you that in Isaiah 54:17 you said that no weapon formed would prosper against me. Thank you in the name of your Son Jesus the Anointed One."

So now, if Bill stops attacking us God will bless him. However, if Bill attempts to attack us, he will run up against God's protective hand.

What gives us the right to expect God to change things for our benefit? What gives Jesus the power to govern in this earth, considering God gave it to Adam, and Adam gave it to Satan? Why is Jesus now in control and authority?

> *Galatians 3:13 Christ hath redeemed us from the curse of the law, being made a curse for us: for it is written, Cursed is every one that hangeth on a tree:*
>
> *Galatians 3:26-29 For ye are all the children of God by faith in Christ Jesus. For as many of you as have*

From Your Lips To God's Ear

been baptized into Christ have put on Christ. There is neither Jew nor Greek, there is neither bond nor free, there is neither male nor female: for ye are all one in Christ Jesus. And if ye be Christ's, then are ye Abraham's seed, and heirs according to the promise.

Luke 13:15-17 The Lord then answered him, and said, Thou hypocrite, doth not each one of you on the sabbath loose his ox or his ass from the stall, and lead him away to watering? And ought not this woman, being a daughter of Abraham, whom Satan hath bound, lo, these eighteen years, be loosed from this bond on the sabbath day? And when he had said these things, all his adversaries were ashamed: and all the people rejoiced for all the glorious things that were done by him.

Psalm 8:1-9 O Lord our Lord, how excellent is thy name in all the earth: who hast set thy glory above the heavens. Out of the mouth of

From Your Lips To God's Ear

babes and sucklings hast thou ordained strength because of thine enemies, that thou mightest still the enemy and the avenger. When I consider thy heavens, the work of thy fingers, the moon and the stars, which thou hast ordained; What is man, that thou art mindful of him? and the son of man, that thou visitest him? For thou hast made him a little lower than the angels, and hast crowned him with glory and honour. Thou madest him to have dominion over the works of thy hands; thou hast put all things under his feet: All sheep and oxen, yea, and the beasts of the field; The foul of the air, and the fish of the sea, and whatsoever passeth through the paths of the seas. O Lord our Lord, how excellent is thy name in all the earth!

We are Heard

Does God really hear us? What evidence do we have that God will hear our prayers?

1 Pet 3:12-15 For the eyes of the

by Dr. Ralph Stowe

From Your Lips To God's Ear

Lord are over the righteous, and his ears are open unto their prayers: but the face of the Lord is against them that do evil. And who is he that will harm you, if ye be followers of that which is good? But and if ye suffer for righteousness' sake, happy are ye: and be not afraid of their terror, neither be troubled; But sanctify the Lord God in your hearts: and be ready always to give an answer to every man that asketh you a reason of the hope that is in you with meekness and fear:

Regardless of our background God will answer our prayers as if they came straight from His Son Jesus the Anointed One if we have faith.

Rom 4:16-17 Therefore it is of faith, that it might be by grace; to the end the promise might be sure to all the seed; not to that only which is of the law, but to that also which is of the faith of Abraham; who is the father of us all, (As it is written, I have made thee a father of many nations,) before him whom he believed, even God, who

From Your Lips To God's Ear

quickeneth the dead, and calleth those things which be not as though they were.

Rom 5:15-21 But not as the offence, so also is the free gift. For if through the offence of one many be dead, much more the grace of God, and the gift by grace, which is by one man, Jesus Christ, hath abounded unto many. And not as it was by one that sinned, so is the gift: for the judgment was by one to condemnation, but the free gift is of many offences unto justification. For if by one man's offence death reigned by one; much more they which receive abundance of grace and of the gift of righteousness shall reign in life by one, Jesus Christ.) Therefore as by the offence of one judgment came upon all men to condemnation; even so by the righteousness of one the free gift came upon all men unto justification of life. For as by one man's disobedience many were made sinners, so by the obedience of one shall many be made righteous.

From Your Lips To God's Ear

> *Moreover the law entered, that the offence might abound. But where sin abounded, grace did much more abound: That as sin hath reigned unto death, even so might grace reign through righteousness unto eternal life by Jesus Christ our Lord.*

We have Redeemed Power

Jesus purchased back what Adam had yielded up to Satan by his transgression. We now have inherited <u>all</u> that was given to Adam... and more!

> *John 16:7-15 Nevertheless I tell you the truth; It is expedient for you that I go away: for if I go not away, the Comforter will not come unto you; but if I depart, I will send him unto you. And when he is come, he will reprove the world of sin, and of righteousness, and of judgment: Of sin, because they believe not on me;*
>
> *Of righteousness, because I go to my Father, and ye see me no more; Of judgment, because the prince of this world is judged. I have yet many things to say unto you, but ye cannot bear them now. Howbeit*

by Dr. Ralph Stowe   49

From Your Lips To God's Ear

when he, the Spirit of truth, is come, he will guide you into all truth: for he shall not speak of himself; but whatsoever he shall hear, that shall he speak: and he will shew you things to come. He shall glorify me: for he shall receive of mine, and shall shew it unto you. All things that the Father hath are mine: therefore said I, that he shall take of mine, and shall shew it unto you.

John 16:23-24 And in that day ye shall ask me nothing. Verily, verily, I say unto you, Whatsoever ye shall ask the Father in my name, he will give it you. Hitherto have ye asked nothing in my name: ask, and ye shall receive, that your joy may be full.

Notice that Jesus has given us the weapons of our warfare. The weapons are the Word, the Name of Jesus, and the Power of the Holy Ghost.

The devil will be here until the time of lease on this earth is complete. When Jesus returns Satan will be bound for one thousand years,

From Your Lips To God's Ear

then released for a time before being cast into that bottomless pit. Adam's lease appears to have been for seven thousand years (sometimes referred to as the seven dispensations). Because God is bound by His Word, He gave authority to Adam, so God does not have the right to just come storming in helping us. Adam, by obedience to Satan, gave authority to Satan. Jesus has purchased that authority back for us. But we now can also choose whom we give authority to.... Satan or God. Our spoken prayer is a tool to release God so that He can enter in. Prayer is based upon what God has already said. This gives God the right to act.

> *John 16:23-24 And in that day ye shall ask me nothing. Verily, verily, I say unto you, Whatsoever ye shall ask the Father in my name, he will give it you. Hitherto have ye asked nothing in my name: ask, and ye shall receive, that your joy may be full.*

> *Philippians 2:9-11 Wherefore God also hath highly exalted him, and given him a name which is above every name: That at the name of Jesus every knee should bow, of things in heaven, and things in*

From Your Lips To God's Ear

earth, and things under the earth; And that every tongue should confess that Jesus Christ is Lord, to the glory of God the Father.

Eph 3:13-19 Wherefore I desire that ye faint not at my tribulations for you, which is your glory. For this cause I bow my knees unto the Father of our Lord Jesus Christ, Of whom the whole family in heaven and earth is named, That he would grant you, according to the riches of his glory, to be strengthened with might by his Spirit in the inner man; That Christ may dwell in your hearts by faith; that ye, being rooted and grounded in love, May be able to comprehend with all saints what is the breadth, and length, and depth, and height; And to know the love of Christ, which passeth knowledge, that ye might be filled with all the fulness of God.

I John 3:23-24 And this is his commandment, That we should believe on the name of His son Jesus Christ, and love one another, as he

From Your Lips To God's Ear

gave us commandment. And he that keepeth his commandments dwelleth in him, and he in him. And hereby we know that he abideth in us, by the Spirit which he hath given us.

Foundation of Every Christian Endeavor

Prayer is the foundation of every Christian endeavor. When we are rooted and grounded in love, we are guaranteed the working knowledge.

Ephesians 3: 12-21 In whom we have boldness and access with confidence by the faith of him. Wherefore I desire that ye faint not at my tribulations for you, which is your glory. For this cause I bow my knees unto the Father of our Lord Jesus Christ, Of whom the whole family in heaven and earth is named, That he would grant you, according to the riches of his glory, to be strengthened with might by his Spirit in the inner man; That Christ may dwell in your hearts by faith; that ye, being rooted and

From Your Lips To God's Ear

> *grounded in love, May be able to comprehend with all saints what is the breadth, and length, and depth, and height; And to know the love of Christ, which passeth knowledge, that ye might be filled with all the fulness of God. Now unto him that is able to do exceeding abundantly above all that we ask or think, according to the power that worketh in us, Unto him be glory in the church by Christ Jesus throughout all ages, world without end. Amen.*

We must remember that prayer is not trying to get God's attention! Nothing escapes God's attention.

> *Hebrews 4:12-16 For the word of God is quick, and powerful, and sharper than any two edged sword, piercing even to the dividing asunder of soul and spirit, and of the joints and marrow, and is a discerner of the thoughts and intents of the heart. Neither is there any creature that is not manifest in His sight: but all things are naked and opened unto the eyes of Him with whom we have to do.*

From Your Lips To God's Ear

> *Seeing then that we have a great High Priest, that is passed into the heavens, Jesus the Son of God, let us hold fast our profession. For we have not an High Priest which cannot be touched with the feeling of our infirmities: but was in all points tempted like as we are, yet without sin. Let us therefore come boldly unto the throne of grace, that we may obtain mercy, and find grace to help in time of need.*

We do not always need to fast nor do we need to whip ourselves nor do we need to rip our clothes nor do we need to put ashes upon our head to pray because Jesus did all of our suffering for us. God has already done all He needs to do. We need to recognize, accept, and act upon His Word.

> *I Peter 4:1 Forasmuch then as Christ hath suffered for us in the flesh, arm yourselves likewise with the same mind: for he that hath suffered in the flesh hath ceased from sin:*

Prayer is not trying to get God to do something! We are not trying to get God to do something. He has already done it all and has stated in His

From Your Lips To God's Ear

Word what He wants to do for us, if we will allow Him to act. Jesus purchased our salvation and our redemption from the curse of the law, and restored us back to the benefits of Adam. No disease. No lack. We have been restored to having dominion over the earth, over every creepy crawly thing, over our enemies, over our flesh.

> *Gal 3:13 Christ hath redeemed us from the curse of the law, being made a curse for us: for it is written, Cursed is every one that hangeth on a tree:*

Prayer is verbal communication with God, believing and receiving what He has already given to us in Christ Jesus! We did not have to beg God to save us, so why would we expect to beg Him for any of the other blessings or benefits He has stated in His Word.

> *Romans 10:6-10 But the righteousness which is of faith speaketh on this wise, SAY NOT IN THINE HEART, WHO SHALL ASCEND INTO THE HEAVEN? (that is, to bring Christ down from above:) Or, Who shall descend into the deep? (that is, to bring up Christ again from the*

From Your Lips To God's Ear

dead:) But what saith it? The Word is nigh thee, even in thy mouth, and in thy heart: that is, the Word of faith, which we preach: That if thou shalt confess with thy mouth the Lord Jesus, and shalt believe in thine heart that God hath raised Him from the dead, thou shalt be saved. For with the heart man believeth unto righteousness; and with the mouth confession is made unto salvation.

The Word is near us, even in our mouths!

From Your Lips To God's Ear

Kinds of Prayer

Jesus spoke a parable directing us to pray so that we may have what we ask. We are to always pray.

Luke 18:1-14 And he spake a parable unto them to this end, that men ought always to pray, and not to faint; Saying, There was in a city a judge, which feared not God, neither regarded man: And there was a widow in that city; and she came unto him, saying, Avenge me of mine adversary. And he would not for a while: but afterward he said within himself, Though I fear not God, nor regard man; Yet because this widow troubleth me, I will avenge her, lest by her continual coming she weary me. And the Lord said, Hear what the unjust judge saith. And shall not God avenge his own elect, which cry day and night unto him, though he bear long with them? I tell you that he will avenge them speedily. Nevertheless when the Son of man

From Your Lips To God's Ear

cometh, shall he find faith on the earth? And he spake this parable unto certain which trusted in themselves that they were righteous, and despised others: Two men went up into the temple to pray; the one a Pharisee, and the other a publican. The Pharisee stood and prayed thus with himself, God, I thank thee, that I am not as other men are, extortioners, unjust, adulterers, or even as this publican.

I fast twice in the week, I give tithes of all that I possess. And the publican, standing afar off, would not lift up so much as his eyes unto heaven, but smote upon his breast, saying, God be merciful to me a sinner. I tell you, this man went down to his house justified rather than the other: for every one that exalteth himself shall be abased; and he that humbleth himself shall be exalted.

If we do not pray, it is usually because of low self-esteem. We do not think ourselves worthy in the eyes of God. This is true rebellion; it is rejection of God's word and His promises.

by Dr. Ralph Stowe

From Your Lips To God's Ear

We have weapons to change things. Not against people, but against the evil that drives the curse.

> *Ephesians 6: 10-18 Finally, my brethren, be strong in the Lord, and in the power of His might. Put on the whole armour of God, that ye may be able to stand against the wiles of the devil. For we wrestle not against flesh and blood, but against principalities, against powers, against the rulers of the darkness of this world, against spiritual wickedness in high places. Wherefore take unto you the whole armour of God, that ye may be able to withstand in the evil day, and having done all, to stand. Stand therefore, having your loins girt about with truth, and having on the breastplate of righteousness; And your feet shod with the preparation of the gospel of peace, Above all, taking the shield of faith, wherewith ye shall be able to quench all the fiery darts of the wicked. And take the helmet of salvation, and the sword of the*

From Your Lips To God's Ear

Spirit, which is the Word of God: Praying always with all prayer and supplication in the Spirit, and watching thereunto with all perseverance and supplication for all saints:

Matthew 18:1 At the same time came the disciples unto Jesus, saying, Who is the greatest in the kingdom of heaven?

But Jesus had already answered this to the disciples.

Matthew 5:19 Whosoever therefore shall break one of these least commandments, and shall teach men so, he shall be called the least in the kingdom of heaven: but whosoever shall do and teach them, the same shall be called great in the kingdom of heaven.

And He reiterates the answer again:

Matthew 18:2-4 And Jesus called a little child unto him, and set him in the midst of them, And said, Verily I say unto you. Except ye be converted, and become as little children, he shall not enter into the kingdom of heaven. Whosover

From Your Lips To God's Ear

therefore shall humble himself as this little child, the same is greatest in the kingdom of heaven.

John 14:12-14 Verily, verily, I say unto you He that believeth on me, the works that I do shall he do also; and greater works than these shall he do; because I go unto my Father. And whatsoever ye shall ask in my name, that will I do, that the Father may be glorified in the Son. If ye shall ask anything in my name, I will do it.

Nehemiah 9:38 And because of all this we make a sure covenant, and write it; and our princes, Levites, and priests, seal unto it.

So, we know we must pray with different kinds of prayer. We must pray God's words and not think too highly of ourselves, but through Jesus the Anointed One who strengthens us. We know what prayer is and what it is not, but there may be different objectives in our prayers. We now know we are worthy to pray, to talk to God through Jesus' Anointing. We know our prayers will be answered and how

From Your Lips To God's Ear

they will be answered. The answer is in the Word of God because that is what we prayed! We know that writing the prayer down is profitable. Let us look at the various types of prayers that we might offer as we pray ceaselessly.

Prayer that Changes Things

We can pray for ourselves, or we can pray for others. Both require different approaches and 'rules', if you will. We can control ourselves, but we do not have the right to direct others. That means when we pray for them, they could go out and undo the effect by their actions. So we see that we might need to repeat requests for others, but for ourselves we need only to ask once and then to praise and thank God for the answer.

Prayer of Agreement

Agreement comes from the Greek for harmony.

> *Matthew 18:19-20 Again I say unto you, That if two of you shall agree on earth as touching any thing that they shall ask, it shall be done for*

From Your Lips To God's Ear

them of my Father which is in heaven. For where two or three are gathered together in my name, there am I in the midst of them.

Mark 11:24- 25 Therefore I say unto you, What things soever ye desire, when ye pray, believe that ye receive them, and ye shall have them. And when ye stand praying, forgive, if ye have ought against any: that your Father also which is in heaven may forgive you your trespasses.

We need to walk in agreement with God. We are spiritual, mental, and physical. All three need to be in agreement within us too. That does not mean we hope it will come to pass, we need to believe, know, and act as though it has come to pass.

Mark 11: 23 For verily I say unto you, That whosoever shall say unto this mountain, Be thou removed, and be thou cast into the sea; and shall not doubt in his heart, but shall believe that those things which he saith shall come to pass; he shall have whatsoever he saith.

by Dr. Ralph Stowe   64

From Your Lips To God's Ear

A prayer of agreement might be a prayer to 'vaccinate' our family from any disease. The prayer might go something like:

> "In Deuteronomy 28:15-45 your Word says sickness and disease is a curse and in Deuteronomy 28:1-14 are the blessings of the Lord. Galatians 3:13 says Christ has redeemed us from the curse of the law. And so we have been redeemed from the curse of disease. Matthew 8:17 Himself bore our sickness and disease that it might be fulfilled. What soever we ask in the Father's name He will give it us; We set ourselves in agreement that we will not have any disease in this household. We write it down and each of us sign it in agreement, in Jesus name."

There is no try, there is only do or not do. We believe we can do. Now having done this we need to stand. If we falter we might need to later bind Satan against us with respect to disease if we find ourselves developing what could be viewed as a symptom. So that takes us to our next section.

Binding and Loosing
Remember that in Ephesians 3:20 it states [He]

From Your Lips To God's Ear

that is able to do exceeding abundantly above all that we ask or think. It is by His power.

> *Matthew 16:15-19 He saith unto them, But whom say ye that I am? And Simon Peter answered and said, Thou art the Christ, the Son of the living God. And Jesus answered and said unto him, Blessed art thou, Simon Barjona: for flesh and blood hath not revealed it unto thee, but my Father which is in heaven. And I say also unto thee, That thou art Peter, and upon this rock I will build my church; and the gates of hell shall not prevail against it. And I will give unto thee the keys of the kingdom of heaven: and whatsoever thou shalt bind on earth shall be bound in heaven: and whatsoever thou shalt loose on earth shall be loosed in heaven.*

Notice that this is binding spirits and loosing Spirits, not people. It is for us to do here on earth, now.

> *Hebrews 1:13-14 But to which of the angels said he at any time, Sit*

From Your Lips To God's Ear

on my right hand, until I make thine enemies thy footstool? Are they not all ministering spirits, sent forth to minister for them who shall be heirs of salvation?

There are three heavens: where God is; outer space; the atmosphere around the earth. Our words command spirits.

2 Corinthians 12:2-4 I knew a man in Christ above fourteen years ago, (whether in the body, I cannot tell; or whether out of the body, I cannot tell: God knoweth;) such an one caught up to the third heaven. And I knew such a man, (whether in the body, or out of the body, I cannot tell: God knoweth;) How that he was caught up into paradise, and heard unspeakable words, which it is not lawful for a man to utter.

Daniel 10:12-13 Then said he unto me, Fear not Daniel: for from the first day that thou didst set thine heart to understand and to chasten thyself before thy God, thy words were heard, and I am come for thy

From Your Lips To God's Ear

> words. But the prince of the kingdom of Persia withstood me one and twenty days: but, lo, Michael, one of the chief princes, came to help me; and I remained there with the kings of Persia.

Spiritual warfare is real. Satan gets involved!

> Ezekiel 28:11-13 Moreover the word of the Lord came unto me, saying, Son of man, take up a lamentation upon the king of Tyrus, and say unto him, Thus saith the Lord God; Thou sealest up the sun, full of wisdom, and perfect in beauty. Thou hast been in Eden the garden of God;...

But Jesus is the almighty power.

> Ezekiel 8:2 Then I beheld, and lo a likeness as the appearance of fire: from the appearance of his loins even downward, fire; and from his loins even upward, as the appearance of brightness, as the colour of amber.

And we have been given that power.

> Acts 2:1-3 And when the day of Pentecost was fully come, they were all with one accord in one place. And suddenly there came a sound from heaven as of a rushing mighty

From Your Lips To God's Ear

> *wind, and it filled all the house where they were sitting. And there appeared unto them cloven tongues like as of fire, and it sat upon each of them.*

So we have the power of Christ given to us and described here just a little differently. But we have the power. We have the obligation. Yes, obligation. Satan is a defeated foe. We have inherited the power of Jesus, but if we do not exercise it, Satan is still in power. We need to take action against his unlawful exercise of power.

Now let's apply this principle to our finances.

> *2 Corinthians 9:6-7 But this I say, He which soweth sparingly shall reap also sparingly; and he which soweth bountifully shall reap also bountifully. Every man according as he purposeth in his heart, so let him give; not grudgingly, or of necessity: for God loveth a cheerful giver.*

> *Deuteronomy 26:2-3 That thou shalt take of the first of all the fruit of the earth, which thou shalt bring of thy land that the LORD thy God*

From Your Lips To God's Ear

> *giveth thee, and shalt put it in a basket, and shalt go unto the place which the LORD thy God shall choose to place his name there. And thou shalt go unto the priest that shall be in those days, and say unto him, I profess this day unto the LORD thy God, that I am come unto the country which the LORD sware unto our fathers for to give us.*

If you sow sparingly, you will reap sparingly. Our giving is in the form of an offering freely given.

> *2 Corinthians 9:8 And God is able to make all grace abound toward you; that ye, always having all sufficiency in all things, may abound to every good work:*

God gives his bounty liberally.

> *2 Corinthians 9:9 (As it is written, He hath dispersed abroad; He hath given to the poor: His righteousness remaineth forever.*

But we need to tithe and give offering.

> *2 Corinthians 9:10-12 Now he that ministereth seed to the sower both*

From Your Lips To God's Ear

> *minister bread for your food, and multiply your seed sown, and increase the fruits of your righteousness;) Being enriched in every thing to all bountifulness, which causeth through us thanksgiving to God. For the administration of this service not only supplieth the want of the saints, but is abundant also by many thanksgivings unto God;*

Now none of this really works if we rob God by not tithing.

> *Malachi 3:8-12 Will a man rob God? Yet ye have robbed me. But ye say, Wherein have we robbed thee? In tithes and offerings. Ye are cursed with a curse: for ye have robbed me, even this whole nation. Bring ye all the tithes into the storehouse, that there may be meat in mine house, and prove me now herewith, saith the LORD of hosts, if I will not open you the windows of heaven, and pour you out a blessing, that there shall not be room enough to receive it. And I will rebuke the devourer for your sakes, and he*

From Your Lips To God's Ear

shall not destroy the fruits of your ground; neither shall your vine cast her fruit before the time in the field, saith the LORD of hosts. And all nations shall call you blessed: for ye shall be a delightsome land, saith the LORD of hosts.

Hebrews 11:4 By faith Abel offered unto God a more excellent sacrifice than Cain, by which he obtained witness that he was righteous, God testifying of his gifts; and by it he being dead yet speaketh.

We must present ourselves obedient to God.

Ephesians 2:2 Wherein in time past ye walked according to the course of this world, according to the prince of the power of the air, the spirit that now worketh in the children of disobedience:

These things work for only one reason: that God gives to establish his covenant, to preach the gospel, to abound in every good work in order to be the answer to the horrible dying world. Let us look at another possible example:

"Satan, in the name of Jesus, take your hands off my money. I bind you according to

From Your Lips To God's Ear

the prayer of binding and loosing. I loose my money from you in the name of Jesus Christ. In Hebrews 1:13,14 He said "But to which of the angels said he at any time, Sit on my right hand, until, I make thine enemies thy footstool? 14 Are they not all ministering spirits, sent forth to minister for them who shall be heirs of salvation? " Ministering angels, I have planted my seed, I have acted upon the word of the living God. And His word says in 2 Corinthians 9:8 that he abounds to me in all grace, therefore ministering angels according to Matthew 16:19 I loose you in Jesus name to go cause all that God has designated as mine to come into my hands."

People are not your problem. You do not pray against people, they are not the problem. You break the power of the devil that is governing that person and then intercede for that person and remind God that no weapon formed against you shall prosper.

"Now you spirit operating in the life of 'name of person' trying to come against 'issue' I break your power. You cannot come against 'issue'. I pray for 'name'. You cannot come against 'issue' and the things of God. I pray for 'name' and I hold them up

From Your Lips To God's Ear

to you and I pray the lord of the harvest get laborers across their path. In the name of Jesus I come. And I remind you here heavenly Father, that I stand upon Isaiah 54:17 that no weapon formed against me shall prosper."

Notice how the word of God is the prayer. How can we go wrong when we pray God's word? Jesus said He only said and did what He saw the Father say and do. How can we go wrong if we do likewise?

> *John 5:19 Then answered Jesus and said unto them, Verily, verily, I say unto you, The Son can do nothing of himself, but what He seeth the Father do; for what things soever He doeth, these also doeth the Son likewise.*

Intercessory Prayer

An intercessor is someone who approaches through prayer, combating principalities, powers, rulers of darkness, and wicked spirits in heavenly places, on behalf of someone else. Never is it for yourself. It can be for any other person who is not a believer. Intercession is a

From Your Lips To God's Ear

prayer of mercy and compassion.

God is looking for someone to pray His words and allow Him to bless us, our countrymen, and our land.

> *Ezekiel 22: 30 And I sought for a man among them, that should make up the hedge, and stand in the gap before me for the land, that I should not destroy it: but I found none.*

We begin first by praying for the lost.

> *1 Timothy 2:1-4 I exhort therefore, that, first of all, supplications, prayers, intercessions, and giving of thanks be made for all men; For kings, and for all that are in authority; that we may lead a quiet and peaceable life in all godliness and honesty. For this is good and acceptable in the sight of God our Savior; Who will have all men to be saved, and to come unto the knowledge of the truth.*

> *Matthew 9:38 Pray ye therefore the Lord of the harvest, that He will send forth labourers into His*

From Your Lips To God's Ear

harvest.

Jesus came in righteousness. He came to bring salvation. He came with purpose to overcome death and lack.

> *Isaiah 59:16-17 And he saw that there was no man, and wondered that there was no intercessor: therefore his arm brought salvation unto him; and his righteousness, it sustained him. For he put on righteousness as a breastplate, and an helmet of salvation upon his head; and he put on the garments of vengeance for clothing, and was clad with zeal as a cloke.*

Jesus came in righteousness, but we now have that same righteousness given to us to use as God has directed so that He is free to bless.

> *Ephesians 6: 10-18 Finally, my brethren, be strong in the Lord, and in the power of His might. Put on the whole armour of God, that ye may be able to stand against the wiles of the devil. For we wrestle not against flesh and blood, but against principalities, against*

From Your Lips To God's Ear

powers, against the rulers of the darkness of this world, against spiritual wickedness in high places. Wherefore take unto you the whole armour of God, that ye may be able to withstand in the evil day, and having done all, to stand. Stand therefore, having your loins girt about with truth, and having on the breastplate of righteousness; And your feet shod with the preparation of the gospel of peace, Above all, taking the shield of faith, wherewith ye shall be able to quench all the fiery darts of the wicked. And take the helmet of salvation, and the sword of the Spirit, which is the Word of God: Praying always with all prayer and supplication in the Spirit, and watching thereunto with all perseverance and supplication for all saints:

Praying in the Spirit

Sometimes we do not know what we should pray for specifically. Many good intentioned people

From Your Lips To God's Ear

just leave it in God's hands. They feel uncomfortable or even refuse to believe what the Word clearly states. They make-up 'other meanings' or just say 'your will be done'. But how can we address the issues we cannot identify? How can we focus upon the problem that needs God's help? Well, God has thought of that too. He has given us the Holy Spirit to help guide us.

We have two choices. If it is about ourselves we can look to James for the answer.

> *James 1:5-7 If any of you lack wisdom, let him ask of God, that giveth to all men liberally, and upbraideth not; and it shall be given him. But let him ask in faith, nothing wavering. For he that wavereth is like a wave of the sea driven with the wind and tossed. For let not that man think that he shall receive any thing of the Lord. 8 A double minded man is unstable in all his ways.*

And if it is for someone else we can look to Paul for the answer, as he stated it in his letter to the Romans.

> *Romans 8:26-28 Likewise the Spirit also helpeth our infirmities: for we*

From Your Lips To God's Ear

know not what we should pray for as we ought: but the Spirit itself maketh intercession for us with groanings which cannot be uttered.

God does have a caution on our use of praying in the spirit. Corporate prayer should not be in the spirit.

1 Corinthians 14:14-19 For if I pray in an unknown tongue, my spirit prayeth, but my understanding is unfruitful. What is it then? I will pray with the spirit, and I will pray with the understanding also: I will sing with the spirit, and I will sing with the understanding also. Else when thou shalt bless with the spirit, how shall he that occupieth the room of the unlearned say Amen at thy giving of thanks, seeing he understandeth not what thou sayest? For thou verily givest thanks well, but the other is not edified. I thank my God, I speak with tongues more than ye all: Yet in the church I had rather speak five words with my understanding, that by my voice I might teach others also, than ten thousand words in an

From Your Lips To God's Ear
unknown tongue.

Petition and Supplication

When we are directed or choose to pray for non-believing family or for other believers, we give supplication to God as our higher authority.

> *Ephesians 6: 18 Praying always with all prayer and supplication in the Spirit, and watching thereunto with all perseverance and supplication for all saints:*

Thanksgiving and Praise

> *I Thessalonians 5:17-18 Pray without ceasing. In every thing give thanks: for this is the will of God in Christ Jesus concerning you.*
>
> *Psalms 100:4 Enter into His gates with thanksgiving, and into His courts with praise: be thankful unto Him, and bless His name.*
>
> *2 Corinthians 9:10-12 Now he that*

From Your Lips To God's Ear

ministereth seed to the sower both minister bread for your food, and multiply your seed sown, and increase the fruits of your righteousness;) Being enriched in every thing to all bountifulness, which causeth through us thanksgiving to God. For the administration of this service not only supplieth the want of the saints, but is abundant also by many thanksgivings unto God;

1 Timothy 2:1-8 I exhort therefore, that, first of all, supplications, prayers, intercessions, and giving of thanks be made for all men; For kings, and for all that are in authority; that we may lead a quiet and peaceable life in all godliness and honesty. For this is good and acceptable in the sight of God our Savior;4 Who will have all men to be saved, and to come unto the knowledge of the truth.5 For there is one God, and one mediator between God and men, the man Christ Jesus; Who gave himself a ransom for all, to be testified in due

From Your Lips To God's Ear

time. Whereunto I am ordained a preacher, and an apostle, (I speak the truth in Christ, and lie not;) a teacher of the Gentiles in faith and verity. I will therefore that men pray every where, lifting up holy hands, without wrath and doubting.

After our prayer or supplication we are directed to give thanksgiving. The answer is sure, so why should we not give thanks immediately?

Philippians 4:4-9 Rejoice in the Lord always: and again I say, Rejoice. Let your moderation be known unto all men. The Lord is at hand. Be careful for nothing; but in every thing by prayer and supplication with thanksgiving let your request be made known unto God. And the peace of God, which passeth all understanding, shall keep your hearts and minds through Christ Jesus. Finally, brethren, whatsoever things are true, whatsoever things are honest, whatsoever things are just, whatsoever things are pure, whatsoever things are lovely, whatsoever things are of good

From Your Lips To God's Ear

report; if there be any virtue, and if there be any praise, think on these things. Those things, which ye have both learned, and received, and heard, and seen in me do: and the God of peace shall be with you.

Psalms 50:14-15 Offer unto God thanksgiving; and pray thy vows unto the most High: And call upon me in the day of trouble: I will deliver thee, and thou shalt glorify me.

Psalms 50:23 Whoso offereth praise glorifieth me: and to him that ordereth his conversation aright will I shew the salvation of God.

Psalm 9:1-2 I will, praise thee, O Lord, with my whole heart; I will shew forth all thy marvelous works. I will be glad and rejoice in thee: I will sing praise to thy name, O thou most High.

Psalm 63:1-4 O God, thou art my God; early will I seek thee: my soul thirsteth for thee, my flesh longeth

From Your Lips To God's Ear

for thee in a dry and thirsty land, where no water is; To see thy power and thy glory, so as I have seen thee in the sanctuary. Because thy loving kindness is better than life, my lips shall praise thee. Thus will I bless thee while I live: I will lift up my hands in thy name.

United or Congregational **Pray**er

Acts 4:23-25 And being let go, they went to their own company, and reported all that the chief priest and elders had said unto them. And when they heard that, they lifted up their voice to God with one accord, and said, Lord, thou art God, which hast made heaven, and earth, and sea, and all that in them is: Who by the mouth of thy servant David hast said, Why did the heathen rage, and the people imagine vain things?

Acts 26-29 The kings of the earth stood up, and the rulers were gathered together against the Lord, and against his Christ. For of a

From Your Lips To God's Ear

truth against thy holy child Jesus, whom thou hast anointed, both Herod, and Pontius Pilate, with the Gentiles, and the people of Israel, were gathered together, For to do whatsoever thy hand and thy counsel determined before to be done. And now, Lord, behold their threatenings: and grant unto thy servants, that with all boldness they may speak thy word,

Acts 4:30-32 By stretching forth thine hand to heal; and that signs and wonders may be done by the name of thy holy child Jesus. And when they had prayed, the place was shaken where they were assembled together; and they were all filled with the Holy Ghost, and they spake the word of God with boldness. And the multitude of them that believed were of one heart and of one soul: neither said any of them that ought of the things which he possessed was his own; but they had all things common.

Acts 5:12-15 And by the hands of the

From Your Lips To God's Ear

apostles were many signs and wonders wrought among the people; (and they were all with one accord in Solomon's porch. And of the rest durst no man join himself to them: but the people magnified them. And believers were the more added to the Lord, multitudes both of men and women.) Insomuch that they brought forth the sick into the streets, and laid them on beds and couches, that at the least the shadow of Peter passing by might overshadow some of them.

Notice that the Bible tells us that if we pray the word, that signs will result to confirm the word. So if we are not seeing signs, we might want to look at our prayers to find out where we are missing the word... or lacking the faith to believe enough to receive.

Mark 16:19-20 So then after the Lord had spoken unto them, he was received up into heaven, and sat on the right hand of God. And they went forth, and preached everywhere, the Lord working with them, and confirming the word with

From Your Lips To God's Ear

signs following. Amen.

Now take careful note of the fact that in the prayer, no mentions of any specifics of any problem are elaborated. Only a focus on God's Word that is the solution.

> *Acts 4:24 And when they heard that, they lifted up their voice to God with one accord, and said, Lord, thou art God, which hast made heaven, and earth, and sea, and all that in them is:*

And the only thing prayed was God's word.

> *Acts 4:29 And now, Lord, behold their threatenings: and grant unto thy servants, that with all boldness they may speak thy word,*

> *Romans 10:17 So then faith cometh by hearing, and hearing by the word of God.*

Signs do not move the unbeliever toward salvation; they only fill the unbeliever with wonder and amazement. Hearing the word causes belief.

> *Acts 3:10 And they knew that it was he which sat for alms at the*

From Your Lips To God's Ear

Beautiful gate of the temple: and they were filled with wonder and amazement at that which had happened unto him.

Acts 4:4 Howbeit many of them which heard the word believed; and the number of the men was about five thousand.

Praying for the Pastor

2 Corinthians 1:8-12 For we would not, brethren have you ignorant of our trouble which came to us in Asia, that we were pressed out of measure, above strength, insomuch that we despaired even of life: But we had the sentence of death in ourselves, that we should not trust in ourselves but in God which raiseth the dead: Who delivered us from so great a death, and doth deliver: in whom we trust that he will yet deliver us; Ye also helping together by prayer for us, that for the gift bestowed upon us by the

From Your Lips To God's Ear

means of many persons thanks may be given by many on our behalf. For our rejoicing is this, the testimony of our conscience, that in simplicity and godly sincerity, not with fleshly wisdom, but by the grace of God, we have had our conversation in the world, and more abundantly to you-ward.

Romans 15:29-32 And I am sure that, when I come unto you, I shall come in the fullness of the blessing of the gospel of Christ. Now I beseech you, brethren for the Lord Jesus Christ's sake, and for the love of the Spirit, that ye strive together with me in your prayers to God for me; That I may be delivered from them that do not believe in Judea; and that my service which I have for Jerusalem may be accepted of the saints; That I may come unto you with joy by the will of God, and may with you be refreshed,

Philippians 1:18-20 What then? Notwithstanding, every way, whether in pretence, or in truth,

From Your Lips To God's Ear

Christ is preached; and I therein do rejoice, yea, and will rejoice. For I know that this shall turn to my salvation through your prayer, and the supply of the Spirit of Jesus Christ, According to my earnest expectation and my hope, that in nothing I shall be ashamed, but that with all boldness, as always, so now also Christ shall be magnified in my body, whether it be by life or by death.

Pray that the pastor speaks the word boldly.

Colossians 4:2-4 Continue in prayer, and watch in the same with thanksgiving; Withal praying also for us, that God would open unto us a door of utterance, to speak the mystery of Christ, for which I am also in bonds: That I may make it manifest, as I ought to speak.

We need to pray for our pastor to be free from people trying to misinterpret the word and causing strife or wrong teaching.

2 Thessalonians 3:1-2 Finally, brethren, pray for us, that the word of the Lord may have free course,

From Your Lips To God's Ear

> *and be glorified, even as it is with you: And that we may be delivered from unreasonable and wicked men: for all men have not faith.*

Our pastors need to have the strength to preach the word irrespective of congregational 'pressures' that may arise.

> *Ephesians 6:18-20 Praying always with all prayer and supplication in the Spirit, and watching thereunto with all perseverance and supplication for all saints: And for me, that utterance may be given unto me, that I may open my mouth boldly, to make known the mystery of the gospel, For which I am an ambassador in bonds: that therein I may speak boldly, as I ought to speak.*

Dedication and Worship

Anytime dedication to the Lord takes place we pray in expectation of acceptance of our offering. Prayer is one of the ways we can worship our Lord. In fact, the word translated as 'pray' in Job 21:15 means to burn incense in

From Your Lips To God's Ear

worship or to intercede.

> *Revelation 8:3-4 And another angel came and stood at the altar, having a golden censer; and there was given unto him much incense, that he should offer it with the prayers of all saints upon the golden altar which was before the throne. And the smoke of the incense, which came with the prayers of the saints, ascended up before God out of the angel's hand.*

Prayer of Committal

Our putting His Word into action by our prayers glorifies God. We need to commit our words to be His words, we need to believe we get them answered, and when we see things to the contrary we need to cast all our cares over onto Him. We need to commit our cares to Him.

> *John 15:7-9 If ye abide in me, and my words abide in you, ye shall ask what ye will, and it shall be done unto you. Herein is my Father glorified, that ye bear much fruit: so shall ye be my disciples. As the Father hath loved me, so have I*

From Your Lips To God's Ear

loved you: continue ye in my love.

Romans 12:2 And be not conformed to this world: but be ye transformed by the renewing of your mind, that ye may prove what is that good, and acceptable, and perfect, will of God.

Having the Word in us, we use our faith, choose our words to be those of God..... and voila... We have what we say....

Oh, no, do not think that you can blab it and grab it. You cannot force God to do your will. You will have your prayer answered because you are in the will of God and He is faithful and just to perform it!

Now, notice that we cannot wait until we want to pray or have a need to pray for help. No, we must be ready, we must prepare by putting God's Word in our mind and in the front of our thoughts. Now, when a need arises, we simply know how to bind Satan and pray to God to get that which we need.

Hebrews 4:12-16 For the Word of God is quick, and powerful, and

From Your Lips To God's Ear

sharper than any twoedged sword, piercing even to the dividing asunder of soul and spirit, and of the joints and marrow, and is a discerner of the thoughts and intents of the heart. Neither is there any creature that is not manifest in his sight: but all things are naked and opened unto the eyes of him with whom we have to do. Seeing then that we have a great high priest, that is passed into the heavens, Jesus the Son of God, let us hold fast our profession. For we have not an high priest which cannot be touched with the feeling of our infirmities; but was in all points tempted like as we are, yet without sin. Let us therefore come boldly unto the throne of grace, that we may obtain mercy, and find grace to help in time of need.

We are guaranteed that our prayers are answered because we pray in the name of Jesus. So we get results!

Hebrews 3:1-2 Wherefore, holy brethren, partakers of the heavenly calling, consider the Apostle and

From Your Lips To God's Ear

High Priest of our profession, Christ Jesus; Who was faithful to him that appointed him, as also Moses was faithful in all his house.

James 1:22 But be ye doers of the word, and not hearers only, deceiving your own selves.

James 2:14 What doth it profit, my brethren, though a man say he hath faith, and have not works? Can faith save him?

No, we must believe God's Word, we must confess God's Word, we must say God's Words in our prayers... and we are assured the results!

To be afraid to confess that it is done or to act as though it is done before we see the answer is to doubt God's Word.

James 3:17 But the wisdom that is from above is first pure, then peaceable, gentle, and easy to be entreated, full of mercy and good fruits, without partiality, and without hypocrisy.

James 4:17 Therefore to him that

From Your Lips To God's Ear

knoweth to do good, and doeth it not, to him it is sin.

We are in the process of receiving... if we are too ignorant to receive we sin against God! We reject Him. We reject what Jesus has done.

II Corinthians 10:3-7 For though we walk in the flesh we do not war after the flesh: (For the weapons of our warfare are not carnal, but mighty through God to the pulling down of strong holds;) Casting down imaginations, and every high thing that exalteth itself against the knowledge of God and bringing into captivity every thought to the obedience of Christ; And having in a readiness to revenge all disobedience, when your obedience is fulfilled. Do ye look on things after the outward appearance? If any man trust to himself that he is Christ's, Let him of himself think again, that, as he is Christ's, even so are we Christ's.

Proverbs 4:20-23 My son, attend to my words; incline thine ear unto my

From Your Lips To God's Ear

sayings. Let them not depart from thine eyes; keep them in the midst of thine heart. For they are life unto those that find them, and health to all their flesh. Keep thy heart with all diligence; for out of it are the issues of life.

Isaiah 55:8-9 For my thoughts are not your thoughts, neither are your ways my ways, saith the Lord. For as the heavens are higher than the earth, so are my ways higher than your ways, and my thoughts than your thoughts.

Philippians 4:6-7 Be careful for nothing; but in every thing by prayer and supplication with thanksgiving let your requests be made know unto God. And the peace of God, which passeth all understanding, shall keep your hearts and minds through Christ Jesus.

1 Peter 5:5-9 Likewise, ye younger, submit yourselves unto the elder. Yea, all of you be subject one

From Your Lips To God's Ear

to another, and be clothed with humility: for God resisteth the proud, and giveth grace to the humble. Humble yourselves therefore under the mighty hand of God, that he may exalt you in due time: Casting all your care upon him; for he careth for you. Be sober, be vigilant; because your adversary the devil, as a roaring lion, walketh about, seeking whom he may devour: Whom resist stedfast in the faith, knowing that the same afflictions are accomplished in your brethren that are in the world.

by Dr. Ralph Stowe

7 Steps to a Deeper Prayer Life

You must believe you receive to get your prayer answered.

> *Matthew 21:21-22 Jesus answered and said unto them, Verily I say unto you, If ye have faith, and doubt not, ye shall not only do this which is done to the fig tree, but also if ye shall say unto this mountain, Be thou removed, and be thou cast into the sea; it shall be done. And all things, whatsoever ye shall ask in prayer, believing, ye shall receive.*

> *Mark 11:24 Therefore I say unto you, What things soever ye desire; when ye pray, believe that ye receive them and ye shall have them.*

Your prayer must be based upon the word of God. Paul said you must think on the word, each and every day, constantly having God's word in your thoughts and ready to come out

From Your Lips To God's Ear

your mouth.

> *Philippians 4:8 Finally, brethren, whatsoever things are true, whatsoever things are honest, whatsoever things are just, whatsoever things are pure, whatsoever things are lovely, whatsoever things are of good report; if there be any virtue, and if there be any praise, think on these things.*

God told Joshua to not let His word stop coming out of his mouth and he would be successful.

> *Joshua 1:8-9 This book of the law shall not depart out of thy mouth; but thou shalt meditate therein day and night, that thou mayest observe to do according to all that is written therein: for then thou shalt make thy way prosperous, and then thou shalt have good success. Have not I commanded thee? Be strong and of good courage; be not afraid, neither be thou dismayed: for the Lord thy God is with thee whithersoever thou goest.*

> *Proverbs 4:20-22 My son, attend to*

From Your Lips To God's Ear

> *my words; incline thine ear unto my sayings. Let them not depart from thine eyes; keep them in the midst of thine heart. For they are life unto those that find them, and health to all their flesh.*

And we know from John that if we pray God's Words, we are confident He answers them because we keep His commandments and do those things that are pleasing to Him.

> *I John 5:14-15 And this is the confidence that we have in him, that, if we ask anything according to his will, he heareth us; And if we know that he hear us, whatsoever we ask, we know that we have the petitions that we desired of him.*

> *I John 3:22-23 And whatsoever we ask, we received of him, because we keep his commandments, and do those things that are pleasing in his sight. And this is his commandment, That we should believe on the name of His Son Jesus Christ, and love one another, as he gave us commandment.*

by Dr. Ralph Stowe

From Your Lips To God's Ear

Step 1: Conduct of life, to include tithing

Our lives must have the intent of following God's laws, precepts, and statutes. Our heart must be toward pleasing God.

Step 2: Base upon the Word of God

God's word never fails. So, if we pray to God His own Word, He is bound to fulfill our requests and answer our prayers. Satan is even bound by God's Word.

Step 3: Apply faith... confessions and action

We must of course believe we receive, but that belief is only as strong as our actions verify. We must act as if we have already received once we ask God. If we pray for ourselves a second time, we have demonstrated that we did not believe He would answer it the first time. We need only to ask once [except for intercession], and then to thank and praise God for the results... of

by Dr. Ralph Stowe   102

course we can praise more than once!

Step 4: Refuse doubt, fear, and defeat

Our answer will be voided if we doubt, fear, or act as though we have been defeated or refused in our request. Asking in doubt, or saying "If it be your will God..." we are admitting we don't know God's word nor do we know His will.

Step 5: Praise God for the receiving

After we ask in prayer, we need then only to give thanksgiving and praise. This demonstrates confidence and belief that our prayer has been answered.

Step 6: Act as though you have already received

If we ask and then try to get the answer ourselves, whom have we believed in? If we ask and then doubt that we will receive unless God wants it or some condition is met, whose word

From Your Lips To God's Ear

have we believed? We MUST act on faith... when we pray for the water to be parted, that first step into what looks like water is the act of faith, and whose Word are we believing? God's word is forever settled in heaven, and His Word in heaven is what materializes here on earth... but He needs a mouth to say it, and to act in belief.

Step 7: Thanksgiving

Why would we not thank God as soon as we ask, if we truly believed He answers prayer?!

Foundations Review

James 5: 13-16 Is any among you afflicted? Let him pray. Is any merry? Let him sing psalms. 24 Is any sick among you? Let him call for the elders of the church; and let them pray over him, anointing him with oil in the name of the Lord: 15 And the prayer of faith shall save the sick, and the Lord shall raise him up; and if he have committed sins, they shall be forgiven him. 16 Confess your faults one to another, and pray one for another, that ye may be healed. The effectual fervent prayer of a righteous man availeth much.

James 1:2-8 My brethren, count it all joy when ye fall into divers temptations; 3 Knowing this, that the trying of your faith worketh patience. 4 But let patience have her perfect work, that ye may be perfect and entire, wanting nothing. 5 If any of you lack wisdom, let him

From Your Lips To God's Ear

ask of God, that giveth to all men liberally, and upbraideth not; and it shall be given him. 6 But let him ask in faith, nothing wavering. For he that wavereth is like a wave of the sea driven with the wind and tossed. 7 For let not that man think that he shall receive any thing of the Lord. 8 A double minded man is unstable in all his ways.

Mark 11:22-26 And Jesus answering saith unto them, Have faith in God 23 For verily I say unto you, That whosoever shall say unto this mountain, Be thou removed, and be thou cast into the sea; and shall not doubt in his heart, but shall believe that those things which he saith shall come to pass; he shall have whatsoever he saith.24 Therefore I say unto you, What things soever ye desire, when ye pray, believe that ye receive them, and ye shall have them. 25 And when ye stand praying, forgive, if ye have ought against any: that your Father also which is in heaven may forgive you your trespasses. 26 But if ye do not

by Dr. Ralph Stowe   106

From Your Lips To God's Ear

> *forgive, neither will your Father which is in heaven forgive your trespasses.*
>
> *Hebrews 11:1 Now faith is the substance of things hoped for, the evidence of things not seen.*

James said to be a doer of the word. Don't just read it. Don't just hope it is true, but be a doer!

> *James 1:22 But be ye doers of the word, and not hearers only, deceiving your own selves.*
>
> *James 2:17 Even so faith, if it hath not works, is dead, being alone.*

We do not pray for faith. That is not what the prayer of faith is! Jesus' disciples even asked for more faith, and Jesus said that they had it because they did what He had asked. They studied the word. Faith comes by hearing the word of God. They had faith. And, further, to every born again person is given the measure of faith.

> *Luke 17:5 And the apostles said unto the Lord, Increase our faith. 6 And the Lord said. If ye had faith as a*

From Your Lips To God's Ear

grain of mustard seed, ye might say unto this sycamine tree, Be thou plucked up by the root, and be thou planted in the sea; and it should obey you.

Romans 10:17 So then faith cometh by hearing, and hearing by the Word of God.

Romans 12:3 For I say, through the grace given unto me, to every man that is among you, not to think of himself more highly than he ought to think; but to think soberly, according as God hath dealt to every man the measure of faith.

Prayer does not make faith work, Faith makes prayer work…. Say and it will….

A prayer of faith is Saying, Believing you receive it, Speaking to it, And believing, to the point of knowing, what is not seen is done.

We pray the prayer of faith, not the prayer of 'look and see', or the prayer of 'boy I hope so', not the prayer of 'but I will do this just in case'. Faith is relying upon the promise irrespective of

From Your Lips To God's Ear

what you see, even until you die! Just remember what FEAR is, False Evidence Appearing Real.... Not real, just appearing real!

> *1 Thessalonians 5:17 Pray without ceasing.*

To develop your prayer life, you will have to study, you will have to learn, and you will make mistakes, but you must base it upon God's word. Laws exist which will not ever be broken or fail.

You must spend time in the word. You must pray. You must be open to learning from the Holy Spirit. Do not shut him out!

> *1 Thessalonians 5 16-19 See that none render evil for evil unto any man; but ever follow that which is good, both among yourselves, and to all men. Rejoice evermore. Pray without ceasing. In every thing give thanks: for this is the will of God in Christ Jesus concerning you. Quench not the Spirit.*

God is not a respecter of persons.

> *Romans 2:11 For there is no respect of persons with God.*

From Your Lips To God's Ear

Colossians 3:25 But he that doeth wrong shall receive for the wrong which he hath done: and there is no respecter of persons.

1 Peter 1:17 And if ye call on the Father, who without respect of persons judgeth according to every man's work, pass the time of your sojourning here in fear:

John 16:23. 24. 27 And in that day ye shall ask me nothing. Verily, verily, I say unto you, Whatsoever ye shall ask the Father in my name, he will give it you. Hitherto have ye asked nothing in my name: ask, and ye shall receive, that your joy may be full. ... For the Father himself loveth you, because ye have loved me, and have believed that I came out from God.

Mark 11:24 Therefore I say unto you, What things soever ye desire, when ye pray, believe that ye receive them, and ye shall have them.

by Dr. Ralph Stowe   110

From Your Lips To God's Ear

Mark 11:22-23 And Jesus answering saith unto them, Have faith in God For verily I say unto you, That whosoever shall say unto this mountain, Be thou removed, and be thou cast into the sea; and shall not doubt in his heart, but shall believe that those things which he saith shall come to pass; he shall have whatsoever he saith.

Mark 11:24,25 Therefore I say unto you, What things soever ye desire, when ye pray, believe that ye receive them, and ye shall have them. And when ye stand praying, forgive, if ye have ought against any: that your Father also which is in heaven may forgive you your trespasses.

1 Peter 3:1 Likewise, ye wives, be in subjection to your own husbands; that, if any obey not the word, they also may without the word be won by the conversation of the wives;

1 Peter 3:7 Likewise, ye husbands,

From Your Lips To God's Ear

> *dwell with them according to knowledge, giving honour unto the wife, as unto the weaker vessel, and as being heirs together of the grace of life; that your prayers be not hindered.*

The Beginning

We now win because of our exercising the Word! Our words need to be God's Word... out loud, not silent. We know from John 1:1 "In the beginning was the Word, and the Word was with God and the Word was God." And we also know from Genesis 1:3; Genesis 1:6; Genesis 1:9; Genesis 1:11; Genesis 1:14; Genesis 1:20; Genesis 1:25; Genesis 1:26; Etc. 'And God said, ... and God saw that it was good.'

Appendix I: Verses with 'pray'

Verses containing the sequential letters 'pray' (i.e., pray, prayer, praying, prayed) are presented below. The verses have been alphabetized to aid those not familiar with the order of the books in the Bible. To the far right are the numbers assigned by Strong to the originally used word (example the word 'pray' in 1 Chr 17:25 is number 6419) (See Appendix II).

Verse	Text of verse	#
1 Chr 17:25	For thou, O my God, hast told thy servant that thou wilt build him an house: therefore thy servant hath found in his heart to pray before thee.	6 4 1 9
1 Chr 21:17	And David said unto God, Is it not I that commanded the people to be numbered? even I it is that have sinned and done evil indeed; but as for these sheep, what have they done? let thine hand, I pray thee, O LORD my God, be on me, and on my father's house; but not on thy people, that they should be plagued.	4 9 9 4
1 Cor 11:13	Judge in yourselves: is it comely that a woman pray unto God uncovered?	4 3 3 6
1 Cor 11:13	Judge in yourselves: is it comely that a woman pray unto God uncovered?	4 3 3 6

From Your Lips To God's Ear

Verse	Text of verse	#
1 Cor 11:4	Every man praying or prophesying, having his head covered, dishonoureth his head.	4 3 3 6
1 Cor 14:13	Wherefore let him that speaketh in an unknown tongue pray that he may interpret.	4 3 3 6
1 Cor 14:13	Wherefore let him that speaketh in an unknown tongue pray that he may interpret.	4 3 3 6
1 Cor 14:14	For if I pray in an unknown tongue, my spirit prayeth, but my understanding is unfruitful.	4 3 3 6
1 Cor 14:14	For if I pray in an unknown tongue, my spirit prayeth, but my understanding is unfruitful.	4 3 3 6
1 Cor 14:15	What is it then? I will pray with the spirit, and I will pray with the understanding also: I will sing with the spirit, and I will sing with the understanding also.	4 3 3 6
1 Cor 14:15	What is it then? I will pray with the spirit, and I will pray with the understanding also: I will sing with the spirit, and I will sing with the understanding also.	4 3 3 6

by Dr. Ralph Stowe

From Your Lips To God's Ear

Verse	Text of verse	#
1 Cor 7:5	Defraud ye not one the other, except it be with consent for a time, that ye may give yourselves to fasting and prayer; and come together again, that Satan tempt you not for your incontinency.	4 3 3 5
1 Cor 7:5	Defraud ye not one the other, except it be with consent for a time, that ye may give yourselves to fasting and prayer; and come together again, that Satan tempt you not for your incontinency.	4 3 3 5
1 John 5:16	If any man see his brother sin a sin which is not unto death, he shall ask, and he shall give him life for them that sin not unto death. There is a sin unto death: I do not say that he shall pray for it.	2 0 6 5
1 Kings 1:12	Now therefore come, let me, I pray thee, give thee counsel, that thou mayest save thine own life, and the life of thy son Solomon.	4 9 9 4
1 Kings 13:6	And the king answered and said unto the man of God, Intreat now the face of the LORD thy God, and pray for me, that my hand may be restored me again. And the man of God besought the LORD, and the king's hand was restored him again, and became as it was before.	6 4 1 9
1 Kings 14:2	And Jeroboam said to his wife, Arise, I pray thee, and disguise thyself, that thou be not known to be the wife of Jeroboam; and get thee to Shiloh: behold, there is Ahijah the prophet, which told me that I should be king over this people.	4 9 9 4
1 Kings 17:10	So he arose and went to Zarephath. And when he came to the gate of the city, behold, the widow woman was there gathering of sticks: and he called to her, and said, Fetch me, I pray thee, a little water in a vessel, that I may drink.	4 9 9 4

by Dr. Ralph Stowe

From Your Lips To God's Ear

Verse	Text of verse	#
1 Kings 17:11	And as she was going to fetch it, he called to her, and said, Bring me, I pray thee, a morsel of bread in thine hand.	4 9 9 4
1 Kings 17:21	And he stretched himself upon the child three times, and cried unto the LORD, and said, O LORD my God, I pray thee, let this child's soul come into him again.	4 9 9 4
1 Kings 19:20	And he left the oxen, and ran after Elijah, and said, Let me, I pray thee, kiss my father and my mother, and then I will follow thee. And he said unto him, Go back again: for what have I done to thee?	4 9 9 4
1 Kings 2:17	And he said, Speak, I pray thee, unto Solomon the king, (for he will not say thee nay,) that he give me Abishag the Shunammite to wife.	4 9 9 4
1 Kings 2:20	Then she said, I desire one small petition of thee; I pray thee, say me not nay. And the king said unto her, Ask on, my mother: for I will not say thee nay.	4 9 9 4
1 Kings 20:31	And his servants said unto him, Behold now, we have heard that the kings of the house of Israel are merciful kings: let us, I pray thee, put sackcloth on our loins, and ropes upon our heads, and go out to the king of Israel: peradventure he will save thy life.	4 9 9 4
1 Kings 20:32	So they girded sackcloth on their loins, and put ropes on their heads, and came to the king of Israel, and said, Thy servant Ben-ha'dad saith, I pray thee, let me live. And he said, Is he yet alive? he is my brother.	4 9 9 4

From Your Lips To God's Ear

Verse	Text of verse	#
1 Kings 20:32	So they girded sackcloth on their loins, and put ropes on their heads, and came to the king of Israel, and said, Thy servant Ben-ha'dad saith, I pray thee, let me live. And he said, Is he yet alive? he is my brother.	4 9 9 4
1 Kings 20:35	And a certain man of the sons of the prophets said unto his neighbour in the word of the LORD, Smite me, I pray thee. And the man refused to smite him.	4 9 9 4
1 Kings 20:37	Then he found another man, and said, Smite me, I pray thee. And the man smote him, so that in smiting he wounded him.	4 9 9 4
1 Kings 20:7	Then the king of Israel called all the elders of the land, and said, Mark, I pray you, and see how this man seeketh mischief: for he sent unto me for my wives, and for my children, and for my silver, and for my gold; and I denied him not.	4 9 9 4
1 Kings 22:13	And the messenger that was gone to call Micaiah spake unto him, saying, Behold now, the words of the prophets declare good unto the king with one mouth: let thy word, I pray thee, be like the word of one of them, and speak that which is good.	4 9 9 4
1 Kings 22:5	And Jehoshaphat said unto the king of Israel, Inquire, I pray thee, at the word of the LORD to day.	4 9 9 4
1 Kings 8:26	And now, O God of Israel, let thy word, I pray thee, be verified, which thou spakest unto thy servant David my father.	6 4 1 9

by Dr. Ralph Stowe

From Your Lips To God's Ear

Verse	Text of verse	#
1 Kings 8:28	Yet have thou respect unto the prayer of thy servant, and to his supplication, O LORD my God, to hearken unto the cry and to the prayer, which thy servant prayeth before thee to day:	8 6 0 5
1 Kings 8:28	Yet have thou respect unto the prayer of thy servant, and to his supplication, O LORD my God, to hearken unto the cry and to the prayer, which thy servant prayeth before thee to day:	8 6 0 5
1 Kings 8:29	That thine eyes may be open toward this house night and day, even toward the place of which thou hast said, My name shall be there: that thou mayest hearken unto the prayer which thy servant shall make toward this place.	8 6 0 5
1 Kings 8:30	And hearken thou to the supplication of thy servant, and of thy people Israel, when they shall pray toward this place: and hear thou in heaven thy dwelling place: and when thou hearest, forgive.	6 4 1 9
1 Kings 8:33	When thy people Israel be smitten down before the enemy, because they have sinned against thee, and shall turn again to thee, and confess thy name, and pray, and make supplication unto thee in this house:	6 4 1 9
1 Kings 8:35	When heaven is shut up, and there is no rain, because they have sinned against thee; if they pray toward this place, and confess thy name, and turn from their sin, when thou afflictest them:	6 4 1 9
1 Kings 8:38	What prayer and supplication soever be made by any man, or by all thy people Israel, which shall know every man the plague of his own heart, and spread forth his hands toward this house:	8 6 0 5

by Dr. Ralph Stowe 119

From Your Lips To God's Ear

Verse	Text of verse	#

1 Kings 8:42	(For they shall hear of thy great name, and of thy strong hand, and of thy stretched out arm;) when he shall come and pray toward this house;	6 4 1 9
1 Kings 8:44	If thy people go out to battle against their enemy, whithersoever thou shalt send them, and shall pray unto the LORD toward the city which thou hast chosen, and toward the house that I have built for thy name:	6 4 1 9
1 Kings 8:45	Then hear thou in heaven their prayer and their supplication, and maintain their cause.	8 6 0 5
1 Kings 8:48	And so return unto thee with all their heart, and with all their soul, in the land of their enemies, which led them away captive, and pray unto thee toward their land, which thou gavest unto their fathers, the city which thou hast chosen, and the house which I have built for thy name:	6 4 1 9
1 Kings 8:49	Then hear thou their prayer and their supplication in heaven thy dwelling place, and maintain their cause,	8 6 0 5
1 Kings 8:54	And it was so, that when Solomon had made an end of praying all this prayer and supplication unto the LORD, he arose from before the altar of the LORD, from kneeling on his knees with his hands spread up to heaven.	6 4 1 9
1 Kings 8:54	And it was so, that when Solomon had made an end of praying all this prayer and supplication unto the LORD, he arose from before the altar of the LORD, from kneeling on his knees with his hands spread up to heaven.	6 4 1 9

From Your Lips To God's Ear

Verse	Text of verse	#
1 Kings 8:54	And it was so, that when Solomon had made an end of praying all this prayer and supplication unto the LORD, he arose from before the altar of the LORD, from kneeling on his knees with his hands spread up to heaven.	8 6 0 5
1 Kings 9:3	And the LORD said unto him, I have heard thy prayer and thy supplication, that thou hast made before me: I have hallowed this house, which thou hast built, to put my name there for ever; and mine eyes and mine heart shall be there perpetually.	8 6 0 5
1 Pet 4:7	But the end of all things is at hand: be ye therefore sober, and watch unto prayer.	4 3 3 5
1 Pet 4:7	But the end of all things is at hand: be ye therefore sober, and watch unto prayer.	4 3 3 5
1 Sam 1:10	And she was in bitterness of soul, and prayed unto the LORD, and wept sore.	6 4 1 9
1 Sam 1:12	And it came to pass, as she continued praying before the LORD, that Eli marked her mouth.	6 4 1 9
1 Sam 1:26	And she said, Oh my lord, as thy soul liveth, my lord, I am the woman that stood by thee here, praying unto the LORD.	6 4 1 9

From Your Lips To God's Ear

Verse	Text of verse	#
1 Sam 1:27	For this child I prayed; and the LORD hath given me my petition which I asked of him:	6 4 1 9
1 Sam 10:15	And Saul's uncle said, Tell me, I pray thee, what Samuel said unto you.	4 9 9 4
1 Sam 12:19	And all the people said unto Samuel, Pray for thy servants unto the LORD thy God, that we die not: for we have added unto all our sins this evil, to ask us a king.	6 4 1 9
1 Sam 12:19	And all the people said unto Samuel, Pray for thy servants unto the LORD thy God, that we die not: for we have added unto all our sins this evil, to ask us a king.	6 4 1 9
1 Sam 12:23	Moreover as for me, God forbid that I should sin against the LORD in ceasing to pray for you: but I will teach you the good and the right way:	6 4 1 9
1 Sam 14:29	Then said Jonathan, My father hath troubled the land: see, I pray you, how mine eyes have been enlightened, because I tasted a little of this honey.	4 9 9 4
1 Sam 15:25	Now therefore, I pray thee, pardon my sin, and turn again with me, that I may worship the LORD.	4 9 9 4

by Dr. Ralph Stowe

From Your Lips To God's Ear

Verse	Text of verse	#
1 Sam 15:30	Then he said, I have sinned: yet honour me now, I pray thee, before the elders of my people, and before Israel, and turn again with me, that I may worship the LORD thy God.	4 9 9 4
1 Sam 16:22	And Saul sent to Jesse, saying, Let David, I pray thee, stand before me; for he hath found favour in my sight.	4 9 9 4
1 Sam 19:2	But Jonathan Saul's son delighted much in David: and Jonathan told David, saying, Saul my father seeketh to kill thee: now therefore, I pray thee, take heed to thyself until the morning, and abide in a secret place, and hide thyself:	4 9 9 4
1 Sam 2:1	And Hannah prayed, and said, My heart rejoiceth in the LORD, mine horn is exalted in the LORD: my mouth is enlarged over mine enemies; because I rejoice in thy salvation.	6 4 1 9
1 Sam 2:36	And it shall come to pass, that every one that is left in thine house shall come and crouch to him for a piece of silver and a morsel of bread, and shall say, Put me, I pray thee, into one of the priests' offices, that I may eat a piece of bread.	4 9 9 4
1 Sam 20:29	And he said, Let me go, I pray thee; for our family hath a sacrifice in the city; and my brother, he hath commanded me to be there: and now, if I have found favour in thine eyes, let me get away, I pray thee, and see my brethren. Therefore he cometh not unto the king's table.	4 9 9 4
1 Sam 22:3	And David went thence to Mizpeh of Moab: and he said unto the king of Moab, Let my father and my mother, I pray thee, come forth, and be with you, till I know what God will do for me.	4 9 9 4

From Your Lips To God's Ear

Verse	Text of verse	#
1 Sam 23:22	Go, I pray you, prepare yet, and know and see his place where his haunt is, and who hath seen him there: for it is told me that he dealeth very subtilly.	4 9 9 4
1 Sam 25:24	And fell at his feet, and said, Upon me, my lord, upon me let this iniquity be: and let thine handmaid, I pray thee, speak in thine audience, and hear the words of thine handmaid.	4 9 9 4
1 Sam 25:25	Let not my lord, I pray thee, regard this man of Belial, even Nabal: for as his name is, so is he; Nabal is his name, and folly is with him: but I thine handmaid saw not the young men of my lord, whom thou didst send.	4 9 9 4
1 Sam 25:28	I pray thee, forgive the trespass of thine handmaid: for the LORD will certainly make my lord a sure house; because my lord fighteth the battles of the LORD, and evil hath not been found in thee all thy days.	4 9 9 4
1 Sam 25:8	Ask thy young men, and they will shew thee. Wherefore let the young men find favour in thine eyes: for we come in a good day: give, I pray thee, whatsoever cometh to thine hand unto thy servants, and to thy son David.	4 9 9 4
1 Sam 26:11	The LORD forbid that I should stretch forth mine hand against the LORD's anointed: but, I pray thee, take thou now the spear that is at his bolster, and the cruse of water, and let us go.	4 9 9 4
1 Sam 26:19	Now therefore, I pray thee, let my lord the king hear the words of his servant. If the LORD have stirred thee up against me, let him accept an offering: but if they be the children of men, cursed be they before the LORD; for they have driven me out this day from abiding in the inheritance of the LORD, saying, Go, serve other gods.	4 9 9 4

by Dr. Ralph Stowe

From Your Lips To God's Ear

Verse	Text of verse	#
1 Sam 26:8	Then said Abishai to David, God hath delivered thine enemy into thine hand this day: now therefore let me smite him, I pray thee, with the spear even to the earth at once, and I will not smite him the second time.	4 9 9 4
1 Sam 28:22	Now therefore, I pray thee, hearken thou also unto the voice of thine handmaid, and let me set a morsel of bread before thee; and eat, that thou mayest have strength, when thou goest on thy way.	4 9 9 4
1 Sam 28:8	And Saul disguised himself, and put on other raiment, and he went, and two men with him, and they came to the woman by night: and he said, I pray thee, divine unto me by the familiar spirit, and bring me him up, whom I shall name unto thee.	4 9 9 4
1 Sam 3:17	And he said, What is the thing that the LORD hath said unto thee? I pray thee hide it not from me: God do so to thee, and more also, if thou hide any thing from me of all the things that he said unto thee.	4 9 9 4
1 Sam 30:7	And David said to Abiathar the priest, Ahimelech's son, I pray thee, bring me hither the ephod. And Abiathar brought thither the ephod to David.	4 9 9 4
1 Sam 7:5	And Samuel said, Gather all Israel to Mizpeh, and I will pray for you unto the LORD.	6 4 1 9
1 Sam 8:6	But the thing displeased Samuel, when they said, Give us a king to judge us. And Samuel prayed unto the LORD.	6 4 1 9

by Dr. Ralph Stowe

From Your Lips To God's Ear

Verse	Text of verse	#
1 Sam 9:18	Then Saul drew near to Samuel in the gate, and said, Tell me, I pray thee, where the seer's house is.	4 9 9 4
1 Tim 2:8	I will therefore that men pray every where, lifting up holy hands, without wrath and doubting.	9 9 9 9
1 Tim 2:8	I will therefore that men pray every where, lifting up holy hands, without wrath and doubting.	4 3 3 6
1 Tim 4:5	For it is sanctified by the word of God and prayer.	1 7 8 3
1Thes 3:10	Night and day praying exceedingly that we might see your face, and might perfect that which is lacking in your faith?	1 1 8 9
1Thes 5:17	Pray without ceasing.	4 3 3 6
1Thes 5:23	And the very God of peace sanctify you wholly; and I pray God your whole spirit and soul and body be preserved blameless unto the coming of our Lord Jesus Christ.	9 9 9 9

From Your Lips To God's Ear

Verse	Text of verse	#
1Thes 5:25	Brethren, pray for us.	4 3 3 6
2 Chr 18:12	And the messenger that went to call Micaiah spake to him, saying, Behold, the words of the prophets declare good to the king with one assent; let thy word therefore, I pray thee, be like one of theirs, and speak thou good.	4 9 9 4
2 Chr 18:4	And Jehoshaphat said unto the king of Israel, Inquire, I pray thee, at the word of the LORD to day.	4 9 9 4
2 Chr 30:18	For a multitude of the people, even many of Ephraim, and Manasseh, Issachar, and Zebulun, had not cleansed themselves, yet did they eat the passover otherwise than it was written. But Hezekiah prayed for them, saying, The good LORD pardon every one	6 4 1 9
2 Chr 30:27	Then the priests the Levites arose and blessed the people: and their voice was heard, and their prayer came up to his holy dwelling place, even unto heaven.	8 6 0 5
2 Chr 32:20	And for this cause Hezekiah the king, and the prophet Isaiah the son of Amoz, prayed and cried to heaven.	6 4 1 9
2 Chr 32:24	In those days Hezekiah was sick to the death, and prayed unto the LORD: and he spake unto him, and he gave him a sign.	6 4 1 9

by Dr. Ralph Stowe

From Your Lips To God's Ear

Verse	Text of verse	#
2 Chr 33:13	And prayed unto him: and he was intreated of him, and heard his supplication, and brought him again to Jerusalem into his kingdom. Then Manasseh knew that the LORD he was God.	6 4 1 9
2 Chr 33:18	Now the rest of the acts of Manasseh, and his prayer unto his God, and the words of the seers that spake to him in the name of the LORD God of Israel, behold, they are written in the book of the kings of Israel.	8 6 0 5
2 Chr 33:19	His prayer also, and how God was intreated of him, and all his sin, and his trespass, and the places wherein he built high places, and set up groves and graven images, before he was humbled: behold, they are written among the sayings of the seers.	8 6 0 5
2 Chr 6:19	Have respect therefore to the prayer of thy servant, and to his supplication, O LORD my God, to hearken unto the cry and the prayer which thy servant prayeth before thee:	8 6 0 5
2 Chr 6:19	Have respect therefore to the prayer of thy servant, and to his supplication, O LORD my God, to hearken unto the cry and the prayer which thy servant prayeth before thee:	8 6 0 5
2 Chr 6:20	That thine eyes may be open upon this house day and night, upon the place whereof thou hast said that thou wouldest put thy name there; to hearken unto the prayer which thy servant prayeth toward this place.	8 6 0 5
2 Chr 6:24	And if thy people Israel be put to the worse before the enemy, because they have sinned against thee; and shall return and confess thy name, and pray and make supplication before thee in this house;	6 4 1 9

by Dr. Ralph Stowe   128

From Your Lips To God's Ear

Verse	Text of verse	#
2 Chr 6:26	When the heaven is shut up, and there is no rain, because they have sinned against thee; yet if they pray toward this place, and confess thy name, and turn from their sin, when thou dost afflict them;	6 4 1 9
2 Chr 6:29	Then what prayer or what supplication soever shall be made of any man, or of all thy people Israel, when every one shall know his own sore and his own grief, and shall spread forth his hands in this house:	8 6 0 5
2 Chr 6:32	Moreover concerning the stranger, which is not of thy people Israel, but is come from a far country for thy great name's sake, and thy mighty hand, and thy stretched out arm; if they come and pray in this house;	6 4 1 9
2 Chr 6:34	If thy people go out to war against their enemies by the way that thou shalt send them, and they pray unto thee toward this city which thou hast chosen, and the house which I have built for thy name;	6 4 1 9
2 Chr 6:35	Then hear thou from the heavens their prayer and their supplication, and maintain their cause.	8 6 0 5
2 Chr 6:37	Yet if they bethink themselves in the land whither they are carried captive, and turn and pray unto thee in the land of their captivity, saying, We have sinned, we have done amiss, and have dealt wickedly;	2 6 0 3
2 Chr 6:38	If they return to thee with all their heart and with all their soul in the land of their captivity, whither they have carried them captives, and pray toward their land, which thou gavest unto their fathers, and toward the city which thou hast chosen, and toward the house which I have built for thy name:	6 4 1 9

by Dr. Ralph Stowe

From Your Lips To God's Ear

Verse	Text of verse	#
2 Chr 6:39	Then hear thou from the heavens, even from thy dwelling place, their prayer and their supplications, and maintain their cause, and forgive thy people which have sinned against thee.	8 6 0 5
2 Chr 6:40	Now, my God, let, I beseech thee, thine eyes be open, and let thine ears be attent unto the prayer that is made in this place.	8 6 0 5
2 Chr 7:1	Now when Solomon had made an end of praying, the fire came down from heaven, and consumed the burnt offering and the sacrifices; and the glory of the LORD filled the house.	6 4 1 9
2 Chr 7:12	And the LORD appeared to Solomon by night, and said unto him, I have heard thy prayer, and have chosen this place to myself for an house of sacrifice.	8 6 0 5
2 Chr 7:14	If my people, which are called by my name, shall humble themselves, and pray, and seek my face, and turn from their wicked ways; then will I hear from heaven, and will forgive their sin, and will heal their land.	6 4 1 9
2 Chr 7:15	Now mine eyes shall be open, and mine ears attent unto the prayer that is made in this place.	8 6 0 5
2 Cor 1:11	Ye also helping together by prayer for us, that for the gift bestowed upon us by the means of many persons thanks may be given by many on our behalf.	1 1 6 2

by Dr. Ralph Stowe

From Your Lips To God's Ear

Verse	Text of verse	#
2 Cor 13:7	Now I pray to God that ye do no evil; not that we should appear approved, but that ye should do that which is honest, though we be as reprobates.	2 1 7 2
2 Cor 5:20	Now then we are ambassadors for Christ, as though God did beseech you by us: we pray you in Christ's stead, be ye reconciled to God.	1 1 8 9
2 Cor 8:4	Praying us with much intreaty that we would receive the gift, and take upon us the fellowship of the ministering to the saints.	1 1 8 9
2 Cor 9:14	And by their prayer for you, which long after you for the exceeding grace of God in you.	1 1 6 2
2 Kings 1:13	And he sent again a captain of the third fifty with his fifty. And the third captain of fifty went up, and came and fell on his knees before Elijah, and besought him, and said unto him, O man of God, I pray thee, let my life, and the life of these fifty thy servants, be precious in thy sight.	4 9 9 4
2 Kings 18:23	Now therefore, I pray thee, give pledges to my lord the king of Assyria, and I will deliver thee two thousand horses, if thou be able on thy part to set riders upon them.	4 9 9 4
2 Kings 18:26	Then said Eliakim the son of Hilkiah, and Shebna, and Joah, unto Rabshakeh, Speak, I pray thee, to thy servants in the Syrian language; for we understand it: and talk not with us in the Jews' language in the ears of the people that are on the wall.	4 9 9 4

by Dr. Ralph Stowe

From Your Lips To God's Ear

Verse	Text of verse	#
2 Kings 19:15	And Hezekiah prayed before the LORD, and said, O LORD God of Israel, which dwellest between the cherubims, thou art the God, even thou alone, of all the kingdoms of the earth; thou hast made heaven and earth.	6 4 1 9
2 Kings 19:20	Then Isaiah the son of Amoz sent to Hezekiah, saying, Thus saith the LORD God of Israel, That which thou hast prayed to me against Sennacherib king of Assyria I have heard.	6 4 1 9
2 Kings 19:4	It may be the LORD thy God will hear all the words of Rabshakeh, whom the king of Assyria his master hath sent to reproach the living God; and will reprove the words which the LORD thy God hath heard: wherefore lift up thy prayer for the remnant that are left.	8 6 0 5
2 Kings 2:16	And they said unto him, Behold now, there be with thy servants fifty strong men; let them go, we pray thee, and seek thy master: lest peradventure the Spirit of the LORD hath taken him up, and cast him upon some mountain, or into some valley. And he said, Ye shall not send.	4 9 9 4
2 Kings 2:19	And the men of the city said unto Elisha, Behold, I pray thee, the situation of this city is pleasant, as my lord seeth: but the water is naught, and the ground barren.	4 9 9 4
2 Kings 2:2	And Elijah said unto Elisha, Tarry here, I pray thee; for the LORD hath sent me to Bethel. And Elisha said unto him, As the LORD liveth, and as thy soul liveth, I will not leave thee. So they went down to Bethel.	4 9 9 4
2 Kings 2:4	And Elijah said unto him, Elisha, tarry here, I pray thee; for the LORD hath sent me to Jericho. And he said, As the LORD liveth, and as thy soul liveth, I will not leave thee. So they came to Jericho.	4 9 9 4

by Dr. Ralph Stowe   132

From Your Lips To God's Ear

Verse	Text of verse	#
2 Kings 2:6	And Elijah said unto him, Tarry, I pray thee, here; for the LORD hath sent me to Jordan. And he said, As the LORD liveth, and as thy soul liveth, I will not leave thee. And they two went on.	4 9 9 4
2 Kings 2:9	And it came to pass, when they were gone over, that Elijah said unto Elisha, Ask what I shall do for thee, before I be taken away from thee. And Elisha said, I pray thee, let a double portion of thy spirit be upon me.	4 9 9 4
2 Kings 20:2	Then he turned his face to the wall, and prayed unto the LORD, saying,	6 4 1 9
2 Kings 20:5	Turn again, and tell Hezekiah the captain of my people, Thus saith the LORD, the God of David thy father, I have heard thy prayer, I have seen thy tears: behold, I will heal thee: on the third day thou shalt go up unto the house of the LORD.	8 6 0 5
2 Kings 4:10	Let us make a little chamber, I pray thee, on the wall; and let us set for him there a bed, and a table, and a stool, and a candlestick: and it shall be, when he cometh to us, that he shall turn in thither.	4 9 9 4
2 Kings 4:22	And she called unto her husband, and said, Send me, I pray thee, one of the young men, and one of the asses, that I may run to the man of God, and come again.	4 9 9 4
2 Kings 4:26	Run now, I pray thee, to meet her, and say unto her, Is it well with thee? is it well with thy husband? is it well with the child? And she answered, It is well.	4 9 9 4

by Dr. Ralph Stowe   133

From Your Lips To God's Ear

Verse	Text of verse	#
2 Kings 4:33	He went in therefore, and shut the door upon them twain, and prayed unto the LORD.	6 4 1 9
2 Kings 5:15	And he returned to the man of God, he and all his company, and came, and stood before him: and he said, Behold, now I know that there is no God in all the earth, but in Israel: now therefore, I pray thee, take a blessing of thy servant.	4 9 9 4
2 Kings 5:17	And Naaman said, Shall there not then, I pray thee, be given to thy servant two mules' burden of earth? for thy servant will henceforth offer neither burnt offering nor sacrifice unto other gods, but unto the LORD.	4 9 9 4
2 Kings 5:22	And he said, All is well. My master hath sent me, saying, Behold, even now there be come to me from mount Ephraim two young men of the sons of the prophets: give them, I pray thee, a talent of silver, and two changes of garments.	4 9 9 4
2 Kings 5:7	And it came to pass, when the king of Israel had read the letter, that he rent his clothes, and said, Am I God, to kill and to make alive, that this man doth send unto me to recover a man of his leprosy? wherefore consider, I pray you, and see how he seeketh a quarrel against me.	4 9 9 4
2 Kings 6:17	And Elisha prayed, and said, LORD, I pray thee, open his eyes, that he may see. And the LORD opened the eyes of the young man; and he saw: and, behold, the mountain was full of horses and chariots of fire round about Elisha.	4 9 9 4
2 Kings 6:17	And Elisha prayed, and said, LORD, I pray thee, open his eyes, that he may see. And the LORD opened the eyes of the young man; and he saw: and, behold, the mountain was full of horses and chariots of fire round about Elisha.	6 4 1 9

From Your Lips To God's Ear

Verse	Text of verse	#
2 Kings 6:18	And when they came down to him, Elisha prayed unto the LORD, and said, Smite this people, I pray thee, with blindness. And he smote them with blindness according to the word of Elisha.	4 9 9 4
2 Kings 6:18	And when they came down to him, Elisha prayed unto the LORD, and said, Smite this people, I pray thee, with blindness. And he smote them with blindness according to the word of Elisha.	6 4 1 9
2 Kings 6:2	Let us go, we pray thee, unto Jordan, and take thence every man a beam, and let us make us a place there, where we may dwell. And he answered, Go ye.	4 9 9 4
2 Kings 6:3	And one said, Be content, I pray thee, and go with thy servants. And he answered, I will go.	4 9 9 4
2 Kings 7:13	And one of his servants answered and said, Let some take, I pray thee, five of the horses that remain, which are left in the city, (behold, they are as all the multitude of Israel that are left in it: behold, I say, they are even as all the multitude of the Israelites that are consumed:) and let us send and see.	4 9 9 4
2 Kings 8:4	And the king talked with Gehazi the servant of the man of God, saying, Tell me, I pray thee, all the great things that Elisha hath done.	4 9 9 4
2 Sam 1:4	And David said unto him, How went the matter? I pray thee, tell me. And he answered, That the people are fled from the battle, and many of the people also are fallen and dead; and Saul and Jonathan his son are dead also.	4 9 9 4

From Your Lips To God's Ear

Verse	Text of verse	#
2 Sam 1:9	He said unto me again, Stand, I pray thee, upon me, and slay me: for anguish is come upon me, because my life is yet whole in me.	4 9 9 4
2 Sam 13:13	And I, whither shall I cause my shame to go? and as for thee, thou shalt be as one of the fools in Israel. Now therefore, I pray thee, speak unto the king; for he will not withhold me from thee.	4 9 9 4
2 Sam 13:26	Then said Absalom, If not, I pray thee, let my brother Amnon go with us. And the king said unto him, Why should he go with thee?	4 9 9 4
2 Sam 13:5	And Jonadab said unto him, Lay thee down on thy bed, and make thyself sick: and when thy father cometh to see thee, say unto him, I pray thee, let my sister Tamar come, and give me meat, and dress the meat in my sight, that I may see it, and eat it at her hand.	4 9 9 4
2 Sam 13:6	So Amnon lay down, and made himself sick: and when the king was come to see him, Amnon said unto the king, I pray thee, let Tamar my sister come, and make me a couple of cakes in my sight, that I may eat at her hand.	4 9 9 4
2 Sam 14:11	Then said she, I pray thee, let the king remember the LORD thy God, that thou wouldest not suffer the revengers of blood to destroy any more, lest they destroy my son. And he said, As the LORD liveth, there shall not one hair of thy son fall to the earth.	4 9 9 4
2 Sam 14:12	Then the woman said, Let thine handmaid, I pray thee, speak one word unto my lord the king. And he said, Say on.	4 9 9 4

From Your Lips To God's Ear

Verse	Text of verse	#
2 Sam 14:18	Then the king answered and said unto the woman, Hide not from me, I pray thee, the thing that I shall ask thee. And the woman said, Let my lord the king now speak.	4 9 9 4
2 Sam 14:2	And Joab sent to Tekoah, and fetched thence a wise woman, and said unto her, I pray thee, feign thyself to be a mourner, and put on now mourning apparel, and anoint not thyself with oil, but be as a woman that had a long time mourned for the dead:	4 9 9 4
2 Sam 15:31	And one told David, saying, Ahithophel is among the conspirators with Absalom. And David said, O LORD, I pray thee, turn the counsel of Ahithophel into foolishness.	4 9 9 4
2 Sam 15:7	And it came to pass after forty years, that Absalom said unto the king, I pray thee, let me go and pay my vow, which I have vowed unto the LORD, in Hebron.	4 9 9 4
2 Sam 16:9	Then said Abishai the son of Zeruiah unto the king, Why should this dead dog curse my lord the king? let me go over, I pray thee, and take off his head.	4 9 9 4
2 Sam 18:22	Then said Ahimaaz the son of Zadok yet again to Joab, But howsoever, let me, I pray thee, also run after Cushi. And Joab said, Wherefore wilt thou run, my son, seeing that thou hast no tidings ready?	4 9 9 4
2 Sam 19:37	Let thy servant, I pray thee, turn back again, that I may die in mine own city, and be buried by the grave of my father and of my mother. But behold thy servant Chimham; let him go over with my lord the king; and do to him what shall seem good unto thee.	4 9 9 4

by Dr. Ralph Stowe

From Your Lips To God's Ear

Verse	Text of verse	#
2 Sam 20:16	Then cried a wise woman out of the city, Hear, hear; say, I pray you, unto Joab, Come near hither, that I may speak with thee.	4 9 9 4
2 Sam 24:17	And David spake unto the LORD when he saw the angel that smote the people, and said, Lo, I have sinned, and I have done wickedly: but these sheep, what have they done? let thine hand, I pray thee, be against me, and against my father's house.	4 9 9 4
2 Sam 7:27	For thou, O LORD of hosts, God of Israel, hast revealed to thy servant, saying, I will build thee an house: therefore hath thy servant found in his heart to pray this prayer unto thee.	6 4 1 9
2 Sam 7:27	For thou, O LORD of hosts, God of Israel, hast revealed to thy servant, saying, I will build thee an house: therefore hath thy servant found in his heart to pray this prayer unto thee.	8 6 0 5
2 Th 1:11	Wherefore also we pray always for you, that our God would count you worthy of this calling, and fulfil all the good pleasure of his goodness, and the work of faith with power:	4 3 3 6
2 Th 3:1	Finally, brethren, pray for us, that the word of the Lord may have free course, and be glorified, even as it is with you:	4 3 3 6
2 Tim 4:16	At my first answer no man stood with me, but all men forsook me: I pray God that it may not be laid to their charge.	9 9 9 9

by Dr. Ralph Stowe

From Your Lips To God's Ear

Verse	Text of verse	#
Acts 1:14	These all continued with one accord in prayer and supplication, with the women, and Mary the mother of Jesus, and with his brethren.	4 3 3 5
Acts 1:24	And they prayed, and said, Thou, Lord, which knowest the hearts of all men, shew whether of these two thou hast chosen,	4 3 3 6
Acts 10:2	A devout man, and one that feared God with all his house, which gave much alms to the people, and prayed to God alway.	1 1 8 9
Acts 10:30	And Cornelius said, Four days ago I was fasting until this hour; and at the ninth hour I prayed in my house, and, behold, a man stood before me in bright clothing,	4 3 3 6
Acts 10:31	And said, Cornelius, thy prayer is heard, and thine alms are had in remembrance in the sight of God.	4 3 3 5
Acts 10:48	And he commanded them to be baptized in the name of the Lord. Then prayed they him to tarry certain days.	2 0 6 5
Acts 10:9	On the morrow, as they went on their journey, and drew nigh unto the city, Peter went up upon the housetop to pray about the sixth hour:	4 3 3 6

From Your Lips To God's Ear

Verse	Text of verse	#

Acts 11:5	I was in the city of Joppa praying: and in a trance I saw a vision, A certain vessel descend, as it had been a great sheet, let down from heaven by four corners; and it came even to me:	4 3 3 6
Acts 12:12	And when he had considered the thing, he came to the house of Mary the mother of John, whose surname was Mark; where many were gathered together praying.	4 3 3 6
Acts 12:5	Peter therefore was kept in prison: but prayer was made without ceasing of the church unto God for him.	4 3 3 5
Acts 13:3	And when they had fasted and prayed, and laid their hands on them, they sent them away.	4 3 3 6
Acts 14:23	And when they had ordained them elders in every church, and had prayed with fasting, they commended them to the Lord, on whom they believed.	4 3 3 6
Acts 16:13	And on the sabbath we went out of the city by a river side, where prayer was wont to be made; and we sat down, and spake unto the women which resorted thither.	4 3 3 5
Acts 16:16	And it came to pass, as we went to prayer, a certain damsel possessed with a spirit of divination met us, which brought her masters much gain by soothsaying:	4 3 3 5

by Dr. Ralph Stowe

From Your Lips To God's Ear

Verse	Text of verse	#
Acts 16:25	And at midnight Paul and Silas prayed, and sang praises unto God: and the prisoners heard them.	4 3 3 6
Acts 16:9	And a vision appeared to Paul in the night; There stood a man of Macedonia, and prayed him, saying, Come over into Macedonia, and help us.	3 8 7 0
Acts 20:36	And when he had thus spoken, he kneeled down, and prayed with them all.	4 3 3 6
Acts 21:5	And when we had accomplished those days, we departed and went our way; and they all brought us on our way, with wives and children, till we were out of the city: and we kneeled down on the shore, and prayed.	4 3 3 6
Acts 22:17	And it came to pass, that, when I was come again to Jerusalem, even while I prayed in the temple, I was in a trance;	4 3 3 6
Acts 23:18	So he took him, and brought him to the chief captain, and said, Paul the prisoner called me unto him, and prayed me to bring this young man unto thee, who hath something to say unto thee.	2 0 6 5
Acts 24:4	Notwithstanding, that I be not further tedious unto thee, I pray thee that thou wouldest hear us of thy clemency a few words.	3 8 7 0

by Dr. Ralph Stowe

From Your Lips To God's Ear

Verse	Text of verse	#
Acts 27:34	Wherefore I pray you to take some meat: for this is for your health: for there shall not an hair fall from the head of any of you.	3 8 7 0
Acts 28:8	And it came to pass, that the father of Publius lay sick of a fever and of a bloody flux: to whom Paul entered in, and prayed, and laid his hands on him, and healed him.	4 3 3 6
Acts 3:1	Now Peter and John went up together into the temple at the hour of prayer, being the ninth hour.	4 3 3 5
Acts 4:31	And when they had prayed, the place was shaken where they were assembled together; and they were all filled with the Holy Ghost, and they spake the word of God with boldness.	1 1 8 9
Acts 6:4	But we will give ourselves continually to prayer, and to the ministry of the word.	4 3 3 5
Acts 6:6	Whom they set before the apostles: and when they had prayed, they laid their hands on them.	4 3 3 6
Acts 8:15	Who, when they were come down, prayed for them, that they might receive the Holy Ghost:	4 3 3 6

by Dr. Ralph Stowe

From Your Lips To God's Ear

Verse	Text of verse	#
Acts 8:22	Repent therefore of this thy wickedness, and pray God, if perhaps the thought of thine heart may be forgiven thee.	1 1 8 9
Acts 8:24	Then answered Simon, and said, Pray ye to the Lord for me, that none of these things which ye have spoken come upon me.	1 1 8 9
Acts 8:34	And the eunuch answered Philip, and said, I pray thee, of whom speaketh the prophet this? of himself, or of some other man?	1 1 8 9
Acts 9:40	But Peter put them all forth, and kneeled down, and prayed; and turning him to the body said, Tabitha, arise. And she opened her eyes: and when she saw Peter, she sat up.	4 3 3 6
Col 1:3	We give thanks to God and the Father of our Lord Jesus Christ, praying always for you,	4 3 3 6
Col 1:9	For this cause we also, since the day we heard it, do not cease to pray for you, and to desire that ye might be filled with the knowledge of his will in all wisdom and spiritual understanding;	4 3 3 6
Col 4:2	Continue in prayer, and watch in the same with thanksgiving;	4 3 3 5

by Dr. Ralph Stowe

From Your Lips To God's Ear

Verse	Text of verse	#
Col 4:3	Withal praying also for us, that God would open unto us a door of utterance, to speak the mystery of Christ, for which I am also in bonds:	4 3 3 6
Dan 6:10	Now when Daniel knew that the writing was signed, he went into his house; and his windows being open in his chamber toward Jerusalem, he kneeled upon his knees three times a day, and prayed, and gave thanks before his God, as he did aforetime.	6 7 3 9
Dan 6:11	Then these men assembled, and found Daniel praying and making supplication before his God.	1 1 5 6
Dan 9:13	As it is written in the law of Moses, all this evil is come upon us: yet made we not our prayer before the LORD our God, that we might turn from our iniquities, and understand thy truth.	2 3 7 0
Dan 9:17	Now therefore, O our God, hear the prayer of thy servant, and his supplications, and cause thy face to shine upon thy sanctuary that is desolate, for the Lord's sake.	8 6 0 5
Dan 9:20	And whiles I was speaking, and praying, and confessing my sin and the sin of my people Israel, and presenting my supplication before the LORD my God for the holy mountain of my God;	6 4 1 9
Dan 9:21	Yea, whiles I was speaking in prayer, even the man Gabriel, whom I had seen in the vision at the beginning, being caused to fly swiftly, touched me about the time of the evening oblation.	8 6 0 5

by Dr. Ralph Stowe   144

From Your Lips To God's Ear

Verse	Text of verse	#
Dan 9:3	And I set my face unto the Lord God, to seek by prayer and supplications, with fasting, and sackcloth, and ashes:	8 6 0 5
Dan 9:4	And I prayed unto the LORD my God, and made my confession, and said, O Lord, the great and dreadful God, keeping the covenant and mercy to them that love him, and to them that keep his commandments;	6 4 1 9
Deut 3:25	I pray thee, let me go over, and see the good land that is beyond Jordan, that goodly mountain, and Lebanon.	4 9 9 4
Deut 9:20	And the LORD was very angry with Aaron to have destroyed him: and I prayed for Aaron also the same time.	6 4 1 9
Deut 9:26	I prayed therefore unto the LORD, and said, O Lord GOD, destroy not thy people and thine inheritance, which thou hast redeemed through thy greatness, which thou hast brought forth out of Egypt with a mighty hand.	6 4 1 9
Eph 6:18	Praying always with all prayer and supplication in the Spirit, and watching thereunto with all perseverance and supplication for all saints;	4 3 3 6
Eph 6:18	Praying always with all prayer and supplication in the Spirit, and watching thereunto with all perseverance and supplication for all saints;	4 3 3 5

by Dr. Ralph Stowe 145

From Your Lips To God's Ear

Verse	Text of verse	#
Exod 10:17	Now therefore forgive, I pray thee, my sin only this once, and intreat the LORD your God, that he may take away from me this death only.	4 9 9 4
Exod 32:32	Yet now, if thou wilt forgive their sin--; and if not, blot me, I pray thee, out of thy book which thou hast written.	4 9 9 4
Exod 33:13	Now therefore, I pray thee, if I have found grace in thy sight, shew me now thy way, that I may know thee, that I may find grace in thy sight: and consider that this nation is thy people.	4 9 9 4
Exod 34:9	And he said, If now I have found grace in thy sight, O Lord, let my Lord, I pray thee, go among us; for it is a stiffnecked people; and pardon our iniquity and our sin, and take us for thine inheritance.	4 9 9 4
Exod 4:13	And he said, O my Lord, send, I pray thee, by the hand of him whom thou wilt send.	4 9 9 4
Exod 4:18	And Moses went and returned to Jethro his father in law, and said unto him, Let me go, I pray thee, and return unto my brethren which are in Egypt, and see whether they be yet alive. And Jethro said to Moses, Go in peace.	4 9 9 4
Exod 5:3	And they said, The God of the Hebrews hath met with us: let us go, we pray thee, three days' journey into the desert, and sacrifice unto the LORD our God; lest he fall upon us with pestilence, or with the sword.	4 9 9 4

by Dr. Ralph Stowe

From Your Lips To God's Ear

Verse	Text of verse	#
Ezek 33:30	Also, thou son of man, the children of thy people still are talking against thee by the walls and in the doors of the houses, and speak one to another, every one to his brother, saying, Come, I pray you, and hear what is the word that cometh forth from the LORD.	4 9 9 4
Ezra 10:1	Now when Ezra had prayed, and when he had confessed, weeping and casting himself down before the house of God, there assembled unto him out of Israel a very great congregation of men and women and children: for the people wept very sore.	6 4 1 9
Ezra 6:10	That they may offer sacrifices of sweet savours unto the God of heaven, and pray for the life of the king, and of his sons.	6 7 3 9
Gen 12:13	Say, I pray thee, thou art my sister: that it may be well with me for thy sake; and my soul shall live because of thee.	4 9 9 4
Gen 13:8	And Abram said unto Lot, Let there be no strife, I pray thee, between me and thee, and between my herdmen and thy herdmen; for we be brethren.	4 9 9 4
Gen 13:9	Is not the whole land before thee? separate thyself, I pray thee, from me: if thou wilt take the left hand, then I will go to the right; or if thou depart to the right hand, then I will go to the left.	4 9 9 4
Gen 16:2	And Sarai said unto Abram, Behold now, the LORD hath restrained me from bearing: I pray thee, go in unto my maid; it may be that I may obtain children by her. And Abram hearkened to the voice of Sarai.	4 9 9 4

by Dr. Ralph Stowe   147

From Your Lips To God's Ear

Verse	Text of verse	#
Gen 18:3	And said, My Lord, if now I have found favour in thy sight, pass not away, I pray thee, from thy servant:	4 9 9 4
Gen 18:4	Let a little water, I pray you, be fetched, and wash your feet, and rest yourselves under the tree:	4 9 9 4
Gen 19:2	And he said, Behold now, my lords, turn in, I pray you, into your servant's house, and tarry all night, and wash your feet, and ye shall rise up early, and go on your ways. And they said, Nay; but we will abide in the street all night.	4 9 9 4
Gen 19:7	And said, I pray you, brethren, do not so wickedly.	4 9 9 4
Gen 19:8	Behold now, I have two daughters which have not known man; let me, I pray you, bring them out unto you, and do ye to them as is good in your eyes: only unto these men do nothing; for therefore came they under the shadow of my roof.	4 9 9 4
Gen 20:17	So Abraham prayed unto God: and God healed Abimelech, and his wife, and his maidservants; and they bare children.	6 4 1 9
Gen 20:7	Now therefore restore the man his wife; for he is a prophet, and he shall pray for thee, and thou shalt live: and if thou restore her not, know thou that thou shalt surely die, thou, and all that are thine.	6 4 1 9

From Your Lips To God's Ear

Verse	Text of verse	#
Gen 23:13	And he spake unto Ephron in the audience of the people of the land, saying, But if thou wilt give it, I pray thee, hear me: I will give thee money for the field; take it of me, and I will bury my dead there.	3 8 6 3
Gen 24:12	And he said, O LORD God of my master Abraham, I pray thee, send me good speed this day, and shew kindness unto my master Abraham.	4 9 9 4
Gen 24:14	And let it come to pass, that the damsel to whom I shall say, Let down thy pitcher, I pray thee, that I may drink; and she shall say, Drink, and I will give thy camels drink also: let the same be she that thou hast appointed for thy servant Isaac; and thereby shall I know that thou hast shewed kindness unto my master.	4 9 9 4
Gen 24:17	And the servant ran to meet her, and said, Let me, I pray thee, drink a little water of thy pitcher.	4 9 9 4
Gen 24:2	And Abraham said unto his eldest servant of his house, that ruled over all that he had, Put, I pray thee, thy hand under my thigh:	4 9 9 4
Gen 24:23	And said, Whose daughter art thou? tell me, I pray thee: is there room in thy father's house for us to lodge in?	4 9 9 4
Gen 24:43	Behold, I stand by the well of water; and it shall come to pass, that when the virgin cometh forth to draw water, and I say to her, Give me, I pray thee, a little water of thy pitcher to drink;	4 9 9 4

by Dr. Ralph Stowe

From Your Lips To God's Ear

Verse	Text of verse	#

Gen 24:45	And before I had done speaking in mine heart, behold, Rebekah came forth with her pitcher on her shoulder; and she went down unto the well, and drew water: and I said unto her, Let me drink, I pray thee.	4 9 9 4
Gen 25:30	And Esau said to Jacob, Feed me, I pray thee, with that same red pottage; for I am faint: therefore was his name called Edom.	4 9 9 4
Gen 27:19	And Jacob said unto his father, I am Esau thy firstborn; I have done according as thou badest me: arise, I pray thee, sit and eat of my venison, that thy soul may bless me.	4 9 9 4
Gen 27:21	And Isaac said unto Jacob, Come near, I pray thee, that I may feel thee, my son, whether thou be my very son Esau or not.	4 9 9 4
Gen 27:3	Now therefore take, I pray thee, thy weapons, thy quiver and thy bow, and go out to the field, and take me some venison;	4 9 9 4
Gen 30:14	And Reuben went in the days of wheat harvest, and found mandrakes in the field, and brought them unto his mother Leah. Then Rachel said to Leah, Give me, I pray thee, of thy son's mandrakes.	4 9 9 4
Gen 30:27	And Laban said unto him, I pray thee, if I have found favour in thine eyes, tarry: for I have learned by experience that the LORD hath blessed me for thy sake.	4 9 9 4

by Dr. Ralph Stowe

From Your Lips To God's Ear

Verse	Text of verse	#
Gen 32:11	Deliver me, I pray thee, from the hand of my brother, from the hand of Esau: for I fear him, lest he will come and smite me, and the mother with the children.	4 9 9 4
Gen 32:29	And Jacob asked him, and said, Tell me, I pray thee, thy name. And he said, Wherefore is it that thou dost ask after my name? And he blessed him there.	4 9 9 4
Gen 33:10	And Jacob said, Nay, I pray thee, if now I have found grace in thy sight, then receive my present at my hand: for therefore I have seen thy face, as though I had seen the face of God, and thou wast pleased with me.	4 9 9 4
Gen 33:11	Take, I pray thee, my blessing that is brought to thee; because God hath dealt graciously with me, and because I have enough. And he urged him, and he took it.	4 9 9 4
Gen 33:14	Let my lord, I pray thee, pass over before his servant: and I will lead on softly, according as the cattle that goeth before me and the children be able to endure, until I come unto my lord unto Seir.	4 9 9 4
Gen 34:8	And Hamor communed with them, saying, The soul of my son Shechem longeth for your daughter: I pray you give her him to wife.	4 9 9 4
Gen 37:14	And he said to him, Go, I pray thee, see whether it be well with thy brethren, and well with the flocks; and bring me word again. So he sent him out of the vale of Hebron, and he came to Shechem.	4 9 9 4

From Your Lips To God's Ear

Verse	Text of verse	#
Gen 37:16	And he said, I seek my brethren: tell me, I pray thee, where they feed their flocks.	4 9 9 4
Gen 37:6	And he said unto them, Hear, I pray you, this dream which I have dreamed:	4 9 9 4
Gen 38:16	And he turned unto her by the way, and said, Go to, I pray thee, let me come in unto thee; (for he knew not that she was his daughter in law.) And she said, What wilt thou give me, that thou mayest come in unto me?	4 9 9 4
Gen 38:25	When she was brought forth, she sent to her father in law, saying, By the man, whose these are, am I with child: and she said, Discern, I pray thee, whose are these, the signet, and bracelets, and staff.	4 9 9 4
Gen 40:14	But think on me when it shall be well with thee, and shew kindness, I pray thee, unto me, and make mention of me unto Pharaoh, and bring me out of this house:	4 9 9 4
Gen 40:8	And they said unto him, We have dreamed a dream, and there is no interpreter of it. And Joseph said unto them, Do not interpretations belong to God? tell me them, I pray you.	4 9 9 4
Gen 44:18	Then Judah came near unto him, and said, Oh my lord, let thy servant, I pray thee, speak a word in my lord's ears, and let not thine anger burn against thy servant: for thou art even as Pharaoh.	4 9 9 4

by Dr. Ralph Stowe

From Your Lips To God's Ear

Verse	Text of verse	#
Gen 44:33	Now therefore, I pray thee, let thy servant abide instead of the lad a bondman to my lord; and let the lad go up with his brethren.	4 9 9 4
Gen 45:4	And Joseph said unto his brethren, Come near to me, I pray you. And they came near. And he said, I am Joseph your brother, whom ye sold into Egypt.	4 9 9 4
Gen 47:29	And the time drew nigh that Israel must die: and he called his son Joseph, and said unto him, If now I have found grace in thy sight, put, I pray thee, thy hand under my thigh, and deal kindly and truly with me; bury me not, I pray thee, in Egypt:	4 9 9 4
Gen 47:29	And the time drew nigh that Israel must die: and he called his son Joseph, and said unto him, If now I have found grace in thy sight, put, I pray thee, thy hand under my thigh, and deal kindly and truly with me; bury me not, I pray thee, in Egypt:	4 9 9 4
Gen 47:4	They said moreover unto Pharaoh, For to sojourn in the land are we come; for thy servants have no pasture for their flocks; for the famine is sore in the land of Canaan: now therefore, we pray thee, let thy servants dwell in the land of Goshen.	4 9 9 4
Gen 48:9	And Joseph said unto his father, They are my sons, whom God hath given me in this place. And he said, Bring them, I pray thee, unto me, and I will bless them.	4 9 9 4
Gen 50:17	So shall ye say unto Joseph, Forgive, I pray thee now, the trespass of thy brethren, and their sin; for they did unto thee evil: and now, we pray thee, forgive the trespass of the servants of the God of thy father. And Joseph wept when they spake unto him.	5 7 7

by Dr. Ralph Stowe

From Your Lips To God's Ear

Verse	Text of verse	#
Gen 50:17	So shall ye say unto Joseph, Forgive, I pray thee now, the trespass of thy brethren, and their sin; for they did unto thee evil: and now, we pray thee, forgive the trespass of the servants of the God of thy father. And Joseph wept when they spake unto him.	4 9 9 4
Gen 50:4	And when the days of his mourning were past, Joseph spake unto the house of Pharaoh, saying, If now I have found grace in your eyes, speak, I pray you, in the ears of Pharaoh, saying,	4 9 9 4
Gen 50:5	My father made me swear, saying, Lo, I die: in my grave which I have digged for me in the land of Canaan, there shalt thou bury me. Now therefore let me go up, I pray thee, and bury my father, and I will come again,	4 9 9 4
Hab 3:1	A prayer of Habakkuk the prophet upon Shigionoth.	8 6 0 5
Hag 2:15	And now, I pray you, consider from this day and upward, from before a stone was laid upon a stone in the temple of the LORD:	4 9 9 4
Heb 13:18	Pray for us: for we trust we have a good conscience, in all things willing to live honestly.	4 3 3 6
Isa 16:12	And it shall come to pass, when it is seen that Moab is weary on the high place, that he shall come to his sanctuary to pray; but he shall not prevail.	6 4 1 9

by Dr. Ralph Stowe   154

From Your Lips To God's Ear

Verse	Text of verse	#
Isa 26:16	LORD, in trouble have they visited thee, they poured out a prayer when thy chastening was upon them.	3 9 0 8
Isa 29:11	And the vision of all is become unto you as the words of a book that is sealed, which men deliver to one that is learned, saying, Read this, I pray thee: and he saith, I cannot; for it is sealed:	4 9 9 4
Isa 29:12	And the book is delivered to him that is not learned, saying, Read this, I pray thee: and he saith, I am not learned.	4 9 9 4
Isa 36:11	Then said Eliakim and Shebna and Joah unto Rabshakeh, Speak, I pray thee, unto thy servants in the Syrian language; for we understand it: and speak not to us in the Jews' language, in the ears of the people that are on the wall.	4 9 9 4
Isa 36:8	Now therefore give pledges, I pray thee, to my master the king of Assyria, and I will give thee two thousand horses, if thou be able on thy part to set riders upon them.	4 9 9 4
Isa 37:15	And Hezekiah prayed unto the LORD, saying,	6 4 1 9
Isa 37:21	Then Isaiah the son of Amoz sent unto Hezekiah, saying, Thus saith the LORD God of Israel, Whereas thou hast prayed to me against Sennacherib king of Assyria:	6 4 1 9

From Your Lips To God's Ear

Verse	Text of verse	#
Isa 37:4	It may be the LORD thy God will hear the words of Rabshakeh, whom the king of Assyria his master hath sent to reproach the living God, and will reprove the words which the LORD thy God hath heard: wherefore lift up thy prayer for the remnant that is left.	8 6 0 5
Isa 38:2	Then Hezekiah turned his face toward the wall, and prayed unto the LORD,	6 4 1 9
Isa 38:5	Go, and say to Hezekiah, Thus saith the LORD, the God of David thy father, I have heard thy prayer, I have seen thy tears: behold, I will add unto thy days fifteen years.	8 6 0 5
Isa 45:20	Assemble yourselves and come; draw near together, ye that are escaped of the nations: they have no knowledge that set up the wood of their graven image, and pray unto a god that cannot save.	6 4 1 9
Isa 5:3	And now, O inhabitants of Jerusalem, and men of Judah, judge, I pray you, betwixt me and my vineyard.	4 9 9 4
Isa 56:7	Even them will I bring to my holy mountain, and make them joyful in my house of prayer: their burnt offerings and their sacrifices shall be accepted upon mine altar; for mine house shall be called an house of prayer for all people.	8 6 0 5
Isa 56:7	Even them will I bring to my holy mountain, and make them joyful in my house of prayer: their burnt offerings and their sacrifices shall be accepted upon mine altar; for mine house shall be called an house of prayer for all people.	8 6 0 5

by Dr. Ralph Stowe

From Your Lips To God's Ear

Verse	Text of verse	#
James 5:13	Is any among you afflicted? let him pray. Is any merry? let him sing psalms.	4 3 3 6
James 5:14	Is any sick among you? let him call for the elders of the church; and let them pray over him, anointing him with oil in the name of the Lord:	4 3 3 6
James 5:15	And the prayer of faith shall save the sick, and the Lord shall raise him up; and if he have committed sins, they shall be forgiven him.	2 1 7 1
James 5:16	Confess your faults one to another, and pray one for another, that ye may be healed. The effectual fervent prayer of a righteous man availeth much.	2 1 7 2
James 5:16	Confess your faults one to another, and pray one for another, that ye may be healed. The effectual fervent prayer of a righteous man availeth much.	1 1 6 2
James 5:17	Elias was a man subject to like passions as we are, and he prayed earnestly that it might not rain: and it rained not on the earth by the space of three years and six months.	4 3 3 6
James 5:18	And he prayed again, and the heaven gave rain, and the earth brought forth her fruit.	4 3 3 6

by Dr. Ralph Stowe

From Your Lips To God's Ear

Verse	Text of verse	#
Jer 11:14	Therefore pray not thou for this people, neither lift up a cry or prayer for them: for I will not hear them in the time that they cry unto me for their trouble.	8605
Jer 14:11	Then said the LORD unto me, Pray not for this people for their good.	6419
Jer 21:2	Inquire, I pray thee, of the LORD for us; for Nebuchadrezzar king of Babylon maketh war against us; if so be that the LORD will deal with us according to all his wondrous works, that he may go up from us.	4994
Jer 29:12	Then shall ye call upon me, and ye shall go and pray unto me, and I will hearken unto you.	6419
Jer 29:7	And seek the peace of the city whither I have caused you to be carried away captives, and pray unto the LORD for it: for in the peace thereof shall ye have peace.	6419
Jer 32:16	Now when I had delivered the evidence of the purchase unto Baruch the son of Neriah, I prayed unto the LORD, saying,	6419
Jer 32:8	So Hanameel mine uncle's son came to me in the court of the prison according to the word of the LORD, and said unto me, Buy my field, I pray thee, that is in Anathoth, which is in the country of Benjamin: for the right of inheritance is thine, and the redemption is thine; buy it for thyself. Then I knew that this was the word of the LORD.	4994

by Dr. Ralph Stowe

From Your Lips To God's Ear

Verse	Text of verse	#
Jer 37:20	Therefore hear now, I pray thee, O my lord the king: let my supplication, I pray thee, be accepted before thee; that thou cause me not to return to the house of Jonathan the scribe, lest I die there.	4 9 9 4
Jer 37:20	Therefore hear now, I pray thee, O my lord the king: let my supplication, I pray thee, be accepted before thee; that thou cause me not to return to the house of Jonathan the scribe, lest I die there.	4 9 9 4
Jer 37:3	And Zedekiah the king sent Jehucal the son of Shelemiah and Zephaniah the son of Maaseiah the priest to the prophet Jeremiah, saying, Pray now unto the LORD our God for us.	6 4 1 9
Jer 37:3	And Zedekiah the king sent Jehucal the son of Shelemiah and Zephaniah the son of Maaseiah the priest to the prophet Jeremiah, saying, Pray now unto the LORD our God for us.	6 4 1 9
Jer 40:15	Then Johanan the son of Kareah spake to Gedaliah in Mizpah secretly, saying, Let me go, I pray thee, and I will slay Ishmael the son of Nethaniah, and no man shall know it: wherefore should he slay thee, that all the Jews which are gathered unto thee should be scattered, and the remnant in Judah perish?	4 9 9 4
Jer 42:2	And said unto Jeremiah the prophet, Let, we beseech thee, our supplication be accepted before thee, and pray for us unto the LORD thy God, even for all this remnant; (for we are left but a few of many, as thine eyes do behold us:)	6 4 1 9
Jer 42:20	For ye dissembled in your hearts, when ye sent me unto the LORD your God, saying, Pray for us unto the LORD our God; and according unto all that the LORD our God shall say, so declare unto us, and we will do it.	6 4 1 9

by Dr. Ralph Stowe

From Your Lips To God's Ear

Verse	Text of verse	#
Jer 42:4	Then Jeremiah the prophet said unto them, I have heard you; behold, I will pray unto the LORD your God according to your words; and it shall come to pass, that whatsoever thing the LORD shall answer you, I will declare it unto you; I will keep nothing back from you.	6 4 1 9
Jer 7:16	Therefore pray not thou for this people, neither lift up cry nor prayer for them, neither make intercession to me: for I will not hear thee.	6 4 1 9
Jer 7:16	Therefore pray not thou for this people, neither lift up cry nor prayer for them, neither make intercession to me: for I will not hear thee.	8 6 0 5
Job 15:4	Yea, thou castest off fear, and restrainest prayer before God.	7 8 8 1
Job 16:17	Not for any injustice in mine hands: also my prayer is pure.	8 6 0 5
Job 21:15	What is the Almighty, that we should serve him? and what profit should we have, if we pray unto him?	6 2 7 9
Job 22:22	Receive, I pray thee, the law from his mouth, and lay up his words in thine heart.	4 9 9 4

by Dr. Ralph Stowe

From Your Lips To God's Ear

Verse	Text of verse	#
Job 22:27	Thou shalt make thy prayer unto him, and he shall hear thee, and thou shalt pay thy vows.	6 2 7 9
Job 32:21	Let me not, I pray you, accept any man's person, neither let me give flattering titles unto man.	4 9 9 4
Job 33:1	Wherefore, Job, I pray thee, hear my speeches, and hearken to all my words.	3 9 9 4
Job 33:26	He shall pray unto God, and he will be favourable unto him: and he shall see his face with joy: for he will render unto man his righteousness.	4 9 9 4
Job 4:7	Remember, I pray thee, who ever perished, being innocent? or where were the righteous cut off?	4 9 9 4
Job 42:10	And the LORD turned the captivity of Job, when he prayed for his friends: also the LORD gave Job twice as much as he had before.	6 4 1 9
Job 42:8	Therefore take unto you now seven bullocks and seven rams, and go to my servant Job, and offer up for yourselves a burnt offering; and my servant Job shall pray for you: for him will I accept: lest I deal with you after your folly, in that ye have not spoken of me the thing which is right, like my servant Job.	6 3 1 9

by Dr. Ralph Stowe

From Your Lips To God's Ear

Verse	Text of verse	#
Job 6:29	Return, I pray you, let it not be iniquity; yea, return again, my righteousness is in it.	4 9 9 4
Job 8:8	For inquire, I pray thee, of the former age, and prepare thyself to the search of their fathers:	4 9 9 4
John 14:16	And I will pray the Father, and he shall give you another Comforter, that he may abide with you for ever;	2 0 6 5
John 16:26	At that day ye shall ask in my name: and I say not unto you, that I will pray the Father for you:	2 0 6 5
John 17:15	I pray not that thou shouldest take them out of the world, but that thou shouldest keep them from the evil.	2 0 6 5
John 17:20	Neither pray I for these alone, but for them also which shall believe on me through their word;	2 0 6 5
John 17:9	I pray for them: I pray not for the world, but for them which thou hast given me; for they are thine.	2 0 6 5

by Dr. Ralph Stowe

From Your Lips To God's Ear

Verse	Text of verse	#
John 17:9	I pray for them: I pray not for the world, but for them which thou hast given me; for they are thine.	2065
John 4:31	In the mean while his disciples prayed him, saying, Master, eat.	2065
Jonah 1:8	Then said they unto him, Tell us, we pray thee, for whose cause this evil is upon us; What is thine occupation? and whence comest thou? what is thy country? and of what people art thou?	4994
Jonah 2:1	Then Jonah prayed unto the LORD his God out of the fish's belly,	6419
Jonah 2:7	When my soul fainted within me I remembered the LORD: and my prayer came in unto thee, into thine holy temple.	8605
Jonah 4:2	And he prayed unto the LORD, and said, I pray thee, O LORD, was not this my saying, when I was yet in my country? Therefore I fled before unto Tarshish: for I knew that thou art a gracious God, and merciful, slow to anger, and of great kindness, and repentest thee of the evil.	577
Jonah 4:2	And he prayed unto the LORD, and said, I pray thee, O LORD, was not this my saying, when I was yet in my country? Therefore I fled before unto Tarshish: for I knew that thou art a gracious God, and merciful, slow to anger, and of great kindness, and repentest thee of the evil.	6419

by Dr. Ralph Stowe

From Your Lips To God's Ear

Verse	Text of verse	#
Josh 2:12	Now therefore, I pray you, swear unto me by the LORD, since I have shewed you kindness, that ye will also shew kindness unto my father's house, and give me a true token:	4 9 9 4
Josh 7:19	And Joshua said unto Achan, My son, give, I pray thee, glory to the LORD God of Israel, and make confession unto him; and tell me now what thou hast done; hide it not from me.	4 9 9 4
Jude 1:20	But ye, beloved, building up yourselves on your most holy faith, praying in the Holy Ghost,	4 3 3 6
Judg 1:24	And the spies saw a man come forth out of the city, and they said unto him, Shew us, we pray thee, the entrance into the city, and we will shew thee mercy.	4 9 9 4
Judg 10:15	And the children of Israel said unto the LORD, We have sinned: do thou unto us whatsoever seemeth good unto thee; deliver us only, we pray thee, this day.	4 9 9 4
Judg 11:17	Then Israel sent messengers unto the king of Edom, saying, Let me, I pray thee, pass through thy land: but the king of Edom would not hearken thereto. And in like manner they sent unto the king of Moab: but he would not consent: and Israel abode in Kadesh.	4 9 9 4
Judg 11:19	And Israel sent messengers unto Sihon king of the Amorites, the king of Heshbon; and Israel said unto him, Let us pass, we pray thee, through thy land into my place.	4 9 9 4

by Dr. Ralph Stowe

From Your Lips To God's Ear

Verse	Text of verse	#
Judg 13:15	And Manoah said unto the angel of the LORD, I pray thee, let us detain thee, until we shall have made ready a kid for thee.	4 9 9 4
Judg 13:4	Now therefore beware, I pray thee, and drink not wine nor strong drink, and eat not any unclean thing:	4 9 9 4
Judg 15:2	And her father said, I verily thought that thou hadst utterly hated her; therefore I gave her to thy companion: is not her younger sister fairer than she? take her, I pray thee, instead of her.	4 9 9 4
Judg 16:10	And Delilah said unto Samson, Behold, thou hast mocked me, and told me lies: now tell me, I pray thee, wherewith thou mightest be bound.	4 9 9 4
Judg 16:28	And Samson called unto the LORD, and said, O Lord GOD, remember me, I pray thee, and strengthen me, I pray thee, only this once, O God, that I may be at once avenged of the Philistines for my two eyes.	4 9 9 4
Judg 16:28	And Samson called unto the LORD, and said, O Lord GOD, remember me, I pray thee, and strengthen me, I pray thee, only this once, O God, that I may be at once avenged of the Philistines for my two eyes.	4 9 9 4
Judg 16:6	And Delilah said to Samson, Tell me, I pray thee, wherein thy great strength lieth, and wherewith thou mightest be bound to afflict thee.	4 9 9 4

by Dr. Ralph Stowe

From Your Lips To God's Ear

Verse	Text of verse	#

Judg 18:5	And they said unto him, Ask counsel, we pray thee, of God, that we may know whether our way which we go shall be prosperous.	4 9 9 4
Judg 19:11	And when they were by Jebus, the day was far spent; and the servant said unto his master, Come, I pray thee, and let us turn in into this city of the Jebusites, and lodge in it.	4 9 9 4
Judg 19:23	And the man, the master of the house, went out unto them, and said unto them, Nay, my brethren, nay, I pray you, do not so wickedly; seeing that this man is come into mine house, do not this folly.	4 9 9 4
Judg 19:6	And they sat down, and did eat and drink both of them together: for the damsel's father had said unto the man, Be content, I pray thee, and tarry all night, and let thine heart be merry.	4 9 9 4
Judg 19:8	And he arose early in the morning on the fifth day to depart: and the damsel's father said, Comfort thine heart, I pray thee. And they tarried until afternoon, and they did eat both of them.	4 9 9 4
Judg 19:9	And when the man rose up to depart, he, and his concubine, and his servant, his father in law, the damsel's father, said unto him, Behold, now the day draweth toward evening, I pray you tarry all night: behold, the day groweth to an end, lodge here, that thine heart may be merry; and to morrow get you early on your way, that thou mayest go home.	4 9 9 4
Judg 4:19	And he said unto her, Give me, I pray thee, a little water to drink; for I am thirsty. And she opened a bottle of milk, and gave him drink, and covered him.	4 9 9 4

by Dr. Ralph Stowe

From Your Lips To God's Ear

Verse	Text of verse	#
Judg 6:18	Depart not hence, I pray thee, until I come unto thee, and bring forth my present, and set it before thee. And he said, I will tarry until thou come again.	4 9 9 4
Judg 6:39	And Gideon said unto God, Let not thine anger be hot against me, and I will speak but this once: let me prove, I pray thee, but this once with the fleece; let it now be dry only upon the fleece, and upon all the ground let there be dew.	4 9 9 4
Judg 8:5	And he said unto the men of Succoth, Give, I pray you, loaves of bread unto the people that follow me; for they be faint, and I am pursuing after Zebah and Zalmunna, kings of Midian.	4 9 9 4
Judg 9:2	Speak, I pray you, in the ears of all the men of Shechem, Whether is better for you, either that all the sons of Jerubbaal, which are threescore and ten persons, reign over you, or that one reign over you? remember also that I am your bone and your flesh.	4 9 9 4
Judg 9:38	Then said Zebul unto him, Where is now thy mouth, wherewith thou saidst, Who is Abimelech, that we should serve him? is not this the people that thou hast despised? go out, I pray now, and fight with them.	4 9 9 4
Lam 1:18	The LORD is righteous; for I have rebelled against his commandment: hear, I pray you, all people, and behold my sorrow: my virgins and my young men are gone into captivity.	4 9 9 4
Lam 3:44	Thou hast covered thyself with a cloud, that our prayer should not pass through.	8 6 0 5

by Dr. Ralph Stowe

From Your Lips To God's Ear

Verse	Text of verse	#
Lam 3:8	Also when I cry and shout, he shutteth out my prayer.	8 6 0 5
Luke 1:10	And the whole multitude of the people were praying without at the time of incense.	4 3 3 6
Luke 1:13	But the angel said unto him, Fear not, Zacharias: for thy prayer is heard; and thy wife Elisabeth shall bear thee a son, and thou shalt call his name John.	1 1 6 2
Luke 10:2	Therefore said he unto them, The harvest truly is great, but the labourers are few: pray ye therefore the Lord of the harvest, that he would send forth labourers into his harvest.	1 1 8 9
Luke 11:1	And it came to pass, that, as he was praying in a certain place, when he ceased, one of his disciples said unto him, Lord, teach us to pray, as John also taught his disciples.	4 3 3 6
Luke 11:1	And it came to pass, that, as he was praying in a certain place, when he ceased, one of his disciples said unto him, Lord, teach us to pray, as John also taught his disciples.	4 3 3 6
Luke 11:2	And he said unto them, When ye pray, say, Our Father which art in heaven, Hallowed be thy name. Thy kingdom come. Thy will be done, as in heaven, so in earth.	4 3 3 6

by Dr. Ralph Stowe

168

From Your Lips To God's Ear

Verse	Text of verse	#
Luke 14:18	And they all with one consent began to make excuse. The first said unto him, I have bought a piece of ground, and I must needs go and see it: I pray thee have me excused.	2065
Luke 14:19	And another said, I have bought five yoke of oxen, and I go to prove them: I pray thee have me excused.	2065
Luke 16:27	Then he said, I pray thee therefore, father, that thou wouldest send him to my father's house:	2065
Luke 18:1	And he spake a parable unto them to this end, that men ought always to pray, and not to faint;	4336
Luke 18:10	Two men went up into the temple to pray; the one a Pharisee, and the other a publican.	4336
Luke 18:11	The Pharisee stood and prayed thus with himself, God, I thank thee, that I am not as other men are, extortioners, unjust, adulterers, or even as this publican.	4336
Luke 19:46	Saying unto them, It is written, My house is the house of prayer: but ye have made it a den of thieves.	4335

by Dr. Ralph Stowe

From Your Lips To God's Ear

Verse	Text of verse	#
Luke 21:36	Watch ye therefore, and pray always, that ye may be accounted worthy to escape all these things that shall come to pass, and to stand before the Son of man.	1 1 8 9
Luke 22:32	But I have prayed for thee, that thy faith fail not: and when thou art converted, strengthen thy brethren.	1 1 8 9
Luke 22:40	And when he was at the place, he said unto them, Pray that ye enter not into temptation.	6 4 1 9
Luke 22:41	And he was withdrawn from them about a stone's cast, and kneeled down, and prayed,	4 3 3 6
Luke 22:44	And being in an agony he prayed more earnestly: and his sweat was as it were great drops of blood falling down to the ground.	4 3 3 6
Luke 22:45	And when he rose up from prayer, and was come to his disciples, he found them sleeping for sorrow,	4 3 3 5
Luke 22:46	And said unto them, Why sleep ye? rise and pray, lest ye enter into temptation.	4 3 3 6

by Dr. Ralph Stowe

From Your Lips To God's Ear

Verse	Text of verse	#
Luke 3:21	Now when all the people were baptized, it came to pass, that Jesus also being baptized, and praying, the heaven was opened,	4 3 3 6
Luke 5:16	And he withdrew himself into the wilderness, and prayed.	4 3 3 6
Luke 5:3	And he entered into one of the ships, which was Simon's, and prayed him that he would thrust out a little from the land. And he sat down, and taught the people out of the ship.	2 0 6 5
Luke 6:12	And it came to pass in those days, that he went out into a mountain to pray, and continued all night in prayer to God.	4 3 3 6
Luke 6:12	And it came to pass in those days, that he went out into a mountain to pray, and continued all night in prayer to God.	4 3 3 6
Luke 6:12	And it came to pass in those days, that he went out into a mountain to pray, and continued all night in prayer to God.	4 3 3 5
Luke 6:28	Bless them that curse you, and pray for them which despitefully use you.	4 3 3 6

by Dr. Ralph Stowe

From Your Lips To God's Ear

Verse	Text of verse	#
Luke 9:18	And it came to pass, as he was alone praying, his disciples were with him: and he asked them, saying, Whom say the people that I am?	4 3 3 6
Luke 9:28	And it came to pass about an eight days after these sayings, he took Peter and John and James, and went up into a mountain to pray.	4 3 3 6
Luke 9:29	And as he prayed, the fashion of his countenance was altered, and his raiment was white and glistering.	4 3 3 6
Mal 1:9	And now, I pray you, beseech God that he will be gracious unto us: this hath been by your means: will he regard your persons? saith the LORD of hosts.	4 9 9 4
Mark 1:35	And in the morning, rising up a great while before day, he went out, and departed into a solitary place, and there prayed.	4 3 3 6
Mark 11:17	And he taught, saying unto them, Is it not written, My house shall be called of all nations the house of prayer? but ye have made it a den of thieves.	4 3 3 5
Mark 11:24	Therefore I say unto you, What things soever ye desire, when ye pray, believe that ye receive them, and ye shall have them.	4 3 3 6

by Dr. Ralph Stowe

From Your Lips To God's Ear

Verse	Text of verse	#
Mark 11:25	And when ye stand praying, forgive, if ye have ought against any: that your Father also which is in heaven may forgive you your trespasses.	4 3 3 6
Mark 13:18	And pray ye that your flight be not in the winter.	4 3 3 6
Mark 13:33	Take ye heed, watch and pray: for ye know not when the time is.	4 3 3 6
Mark 14:32	And they came to a place which was named Gethsemane: and he saith to his disciples, Sit ye here, while I shall pray.	4 3 3 6
Mark 14:35	And he went forward a little, and fell on the ground, and prayed that, if it were possible, the hour might pass from him.	4 3 3 6
Mark 14:38	Watch ye and pray, lest ye enter into temptation. The spirit truly is ready, but the flesh is weak.	4 3 3 6
Mark 14:39	And again he went away, and prayed, and spake the same words.	4 3 3 6

by Dr. Ralph Stowe

From Your Lips To God's Ear

Verse	Text of verse	#
Mark 5:17	And they began to pray him to depart out of their coasts.	3 8 7 0
Mark 5:18	And when he was come into the ship, he that had been possessed with the devil prayed him that he might be with him.	3 8 7 0
Mark 5:23	And besought him greatly, saying, My little daughter lieth at the point of death: I pray thee, come and lay thy hands on her, that she may be healed; and she shall live.	9 9 9 9
Mark 6:46	And when he had sent them away, he departed into a mountain to pray.	4 3 3 6
Mark 9:29	And he said unto them, This kind can come forth by nothing, but by prayer and fasting.	4 3 3 5
Matt 14:23	And when he had sent the multitudes away, he went up into a mountain apart to pray: and when the evening was come, he was there alone.	4 3 3 6
Matt 17:21	Howbeit this kind goeth not out but by prayer and fasting.	4 3 3 5

by Dr. Ralph Stowe

From Your Lips To God's Ear

Verse	Text of verse	#
Matt 19:13	Then were there brought unto him little children, that he should put his hands on them, and pray: and the disciples rebuked them.	4 3 3 6
Matt 21:13	And said unto them, It is written, My house shall be called the house of prayer; but ye have made it a den of thieves.	4 3 3 5
Matt 21:22	And all things, whatsoever ye shall ask in prayer, believing, ye shall receive.	4 3 3 5
Matt 23:14	Woe unto you, scribes and Pharisees, hypocrites! for ye devour widows' houses, and for a pretence make long prayer: therefore ye shall receive the greater damnation.	4 3 3 6
Matt 24:20	But pray ye that your flight be not in the winter, neither on the sabbath day:	4 3 3 6
Matt 26:36	Then cometh Jesus with them unto a place called Gethsemane, and saith unto the disciples, Sit ye here, while I go and pray yonder.	4 3 3 6
Matt 26:39	And he went a little further, and fell on his face, and prayed, saying, O my Father, if it be possible, let this cup pass from me: nevertheless not as I will, but as thou wilt.	4 3 3 6

by Dr. Ralph Stowe

From Your Lips To God's Ear

Verse	Text of verse	#
Matt 26:41	Watch and pray, that ye enter not into temptation: the spirit indeed is willing, but the flesh is weak.	4 3 3 6
Matt 26:42	He went away again the second time, and prayed, saying, O my Father, if this cup may not pass away from me, except I drink it, thy will be done.	4 3 3 6
Matt 26:44	And he left them, and went away again, and prayed the third time, saying the same words.	4 3 3 6
Matt 26:53	Thinkest thou that I cannot now pray to my Father, and he shall presently give me more than twelve legions of angels?	3 8 7 0
Matt 5:44	But I say unto you, Love your enemies, bless them that curse you, do good to them that hate you, and pray for them which despitefully use you, and persecute you;	4 3 3 6
Matt 6:5	And when thou prayest, thou shalt not be as the hypocrites are: for they love to pray standing in the synagogues and in the corners of the streets, that they may be seen of men. Verily I say unto you, They have their reward.	4 3 3 6
Matt 6:6	But thou, when thou prayest, enter into thy closet, and when thou hast shut thy door, pray to thy Father which is in secret; and thy Father which seeth in secret shall reward thee openly.	4 3 3 6

by Dr. Ralph Stowe   176

From Your Lips To God's Ear

Verse	Text of verse	#
Matt 6:7	But when ye pray, use not vain repetitions, as the heathen do: for they think that they shall be heard for their much speaking.	4 3 3 6
Matt 6:9	After this manner therefore pray ye: Our Father which art in heaven, Hallowed be thy name.	4 3 3 6
Matt 9:38	Pray ye therefore the Lord of the harvest, that he will send forth labourers into his harvest.	1 1 8 9
Micah 3:1	And I said, Hear, I pray you, O heads of Jacob, and ye princes of the house of Israel; Is it not for you to know judgment?	4 9 9 4
Micah 3:9	Hear this, I pray you, ye heads of the house of Jacob, and princes of the house of Israel, that abhor judgment, and pervert all equity.	4 9 9 4
Neh 1:11	O Lord, I beseech thee, let now thine ear be attentive to the prayer of thy servant, and to the prayer of thy servants, who desire to fear thy name: and prosper, I pray thee, thy servant this day, and grant him mercy in the sight of this man. For I was the king's cupbearer.	8 6 0 5
Neh 1:11	O Lord, I beseech thee, let now thine ear be attentive to the prayer of thy servant, and to the prayer of thy servants, who desire to fear thy name: and prosper, I pray thee, thy servant this day, and grant him mercy in the sight of this man. For I was the king's cupbearer.	8 6 0 5

by Dr. Ralph Stowe

From Your Lips To God's Ear

Verse	Text of verse	#
Neh 1:11	O Lord, I beseech thee, let now thine ear be attentive to the prayer of thy servant, and to the prayer of thy servants, who desire to fear thy name: and prosper, I pray thee, thy servant this day, and grant him mercy in the sight of this man. For I was the king's cupbearer.	4 9 9 4
Neh 1:4	And it came to pass, when I heard these words, that I sat down and wept, and mourned certain days, and fasted, and prayed before the God of heaven,	6 4 1 9
Neh 1:6	Let thine ear now be attentive, and thine eyes open, that thou mayest hear the prayer of thy servant, which I pray before thee now, day and night, for the children of Israel thy servants, and confess the sins of the children of Israel, which we have sinned against thee: both I and my father's house have sinned.	8 6 0 5
Neh 1:6	Let thine ear now be attentive, and thine eyes open, that thou mayest hear the prayer of thy servant, which I pray before thee now, day and night, for the children of Israel thy servants, and confess the sins of the children of Israel, which we have sinned against thee: both I and my father's house have sinned.	6 4 1 9
Neh 11:17	And Mattaniah the son of Micha, the son of Zabdi, the son of Asaph, was the principal to begin the thanksgiving in prayer: and Bakbukiah the second among his brethren, and Abda the son of Shammua, the son of Galal, the son of Jeduthun.	8 6 0 5
Neh 2:4	Then the king said unto me, For what dost thou make request? So I prayed to the God of heaven.	6 4 1 9
Neh 4:9	Nevertheless we made our prayer unto our God, and set a watch against them day and night, because of them.	6 4 1 9

by Dr. Ralph Stowe   178

From Your Lips To God's Ear

Verse	Text of verse	#
Neh 5:10	I likewise, and my brethren, and my servants, might exact of them money and corn: I pray you, let us leave off this usury.	4 9 9 4
Neh 5:11	Restore, I pray you, to them, even this day, their lands, their vineyards, their oliveyards, and their houses, also the hundredth part of the money, and of the corn, the wine, and the oil, that ye exact of them.	4 9 9 4
Num 10:31	And he said, Leave us not, I pray thee; forasmuch as thou knowest how we are to encamp in the wilderness, and thou mayest be to us instead of eyes.	4 9 9 4
Num 11:15	And if thou deal thus with me, kill me, I pray thee, out of hand, if I have found favour in thy sight; and let me not see my wretchedness.	4 9 9 4
Num 11:2	And the people cried unto Moses; and when Moses prayed unto the LORD, the fire was quenched.	6 4 1 9
Num 16:26	And he spake unto the congregation, saying, Depart, I pray you, from the tents of these wicked men, and touch nothing of theirs, lest ye be consumed in all their sins.	4 9 9 4
Num 16:8	And Moses said unto Korah, Hear, I pray you, ye sons of Levi:	4 9 9 4

by Dr. Ralph Stowe

From Your Lips To God's Ear

Verse	Text of verse	#
Num 20:17	Let us pass, I pray thee, through thy country: we will not pass through the fields, or through the vineyards, neither will we drink of the water of the wells: we will go by the king's high way, we will not turn to the right hand nor to the left, until we have passed thy borders.	4 9 9 4
Num 21:7	Therefore the people came to Moses, and said, We have sinned, for we have spoken against the LORD, and against thee; pray unto the LORD, that he take away the serpents from us. And Moses prayed for the people.	6 4 1 9
Num 21:7	Therefore the people came to Moses, and said, We have sinned, for we have spoken against the LORD, and against thee; pray unto the LORD, that he take away the serpents from us. And Moses prayed for the people.	6 4 1 9
Num 22:16	And they came to Balaam, and said to him, Thus saith Balak the son of Zippor, Let nothing, I pray thee, hinder thee from coming unto me:	4 9 9 4
Num 22:17	For I will promote thee unto very great honour, and I will do whatsoever thou sayest unto me: come therefore, I pray thee, curse me this people.	4 9 9 4
Num 22:19	Now therefore, I pray you, tarry ye also here this night, that I may know what the LORD will say unto me more.	4 9 9 4
Num 22:6	Come now therefore, I pray thee, curse me this people; for they are too mighty for me: peradventure I shall prevail, that we may smite them, and that I may drive them out of the land: for I wot that he whom thou blessest is blessed, and he whom thou cursest is cursed.	4 9 9 4

by Dr. Ralph Stowe

From Your Lips To God's Ear

Verse	Text of verse	#
Num 23:13	And Balak said unto him, Come, I pray thee, with me unto another place, from whence thou mayest see them: thou shalt see but the utmost part of them, and shalt not see them all: and curse me them from thence.	4 9 9 4
Num 23:27	And Balak said unto Balaam, Come, I pray thee, I will bring thee unto another place; peradventure it will please God that thou mayest curse me them from thence.	4 9 9 4
Phil 1:19	For I know that this shall turn to my salvation through your prayer, and the supply of the Spirit of Jesus Christ,	1 1 6 2
Phil 1:4	Always in every prayer of mine for you all making request with joy,	1 1 6 2
Phil 1:9	And this I pray, that your love may abound yet more and more in knowledge and in all judgment;	4 3 3 6
Phil 4:6	Be careful for nothing; but in every thing by prayer and supplication with thanksgiving let your requests be made known unto God.	4 3 3 5
Prov 15:29	The LORD is far from the wicked: but he heareth the prayer of the righteous.	8 6 0 5

by Dr. Ralph Stowe

From Your Lips To God's Ear

Verse	Text of verse	#
Prov 15:8	The sacrifice of the wicked is an abomination to the LORD: but the prayer of the upright is his delight.	8 6 0 5
Prov 28:9	He that turneth away his ear from hearing the law, even his prayer shall be abomination.	8 6 0 5
Ps 4:1	Hear me when I call, O God of my righteousness: thou hast enlarged me when I was in distress; have mercy upon me, and hear my prayer.	8 6 0 5
Ps 5:3	My voice shalt thou hear in the morning, O LORD; in the morning will I direct my prayer unto thee, and will look up.	9 9 9 9
Ps 5:2	Hearken unto the voice of my cry, my King, and my God: for unto thee will I pray.	6 4 1 9
Ps 6:9	The LORD hath heard my supplication; the LORD will receive my prayer.	8 6 0 5
Ps 17:1	Hear the right, O LORD, attend unto my cry, give ear unto my prayer, that goeth not out of feigned lips.	8 6 0 5

by Dr. Ralph Stowe

From Your Lips To God's Ear

Verse	Text of verse	#
Ps 32:6	For this shall every one that is godly pray unto thee in a time when thou mayest be found: surely in the floods of great waters they shall not come nigh unto him.	6 4 1 9
Ps 35:13	But as for me, when they were sick, my clothing was sackcloth: I humbled my soul with fasting; and my prayer returned into mine own bosom.	8 6 0 5
Ps 39:12	Hear my prayer, O LORD, and give ear unto my cry; hold not thy peace at my tears: for I am a stranger with thee, and a sojourner, as all my fathers were.	8 6 0 5
Ps 42:8	Yet the LORD will command his lovingkindness in the daytime, and in the night his song shall be with me, and my prayer unto the God of my life.	8 6 0 5
Ps 54:2	Hear my prayer, O God; give ear to the words of my mouth.	8 6 0 5
Ps 55:1	Give ear to my prayer, O God; and hide not thyself from my supplication.	8 6 0 5
Ps 55:17	Evening, and morning, and at noon, will I pray, and cry aloud: and he shall hear my voice.	7 8 7 8

by Dr. Ralph Stowe   183

From Your Lips To God's Ear

Verse	Text of verse	#
Ps 61:1	Hear my cry, O God; attend unto my prayer.	8605
Ps 64:1	Hear my voice, O God, in my prayer: preserve my life from fear of the enemy.	7879
Ps 65:2	O thou that hearest prayer, unto thee shall all flesh come.	8605
Ps 66:19	But verily God hath heard me; he hath attended to the voice of my prayer.	8605
Ps 102:1	Hear my prayer, O LORD, and let my cry come unto thee.	8605
Ps 102:17	He will regard the prayer of the destitute, and not despise their prayer.	8605
Ps 102:17	He will regard the prayer of the destitute, and not despise their prayer.	8605

From Your Lips To God's Ear

Verse	Text of verse	#
Ps 109:4	For my love they are my adversaries: but I give myself unto prayer.	8 6 0 5
Ps 109:7	When he shall be judged, let him be condemned: and let his prayer become sin.	8 6 0 5
Ps 119:76	Let, I pray thee, thy merciful kindness be for my comfort, according to thy word unto thy servant.	4 9 9 4
Ps 122:6	Pray for the peace of Jerusalem: they shall prosper that love thee.	7 5 9 2
Ps 141:2	Let my prayer be set forth before thee as incense; and the lifting up of my hands as the evening sacrifice.	8 6 0 5
Ps 141:5	Let the righteous smite me; it shall be a kindness: and let him reprove me; it shall be an excellent oil, which shall not break my head: for yet my prayer also shall be in their calamities.	8 6 0 5
Ps 143:1	Hear my prayer, O LORD, give ear to my supplications: in thy faithfulness answer me, and in thy righteousness.	8 6 0 5

From Your Lips To God's Ear

Verse	Text of verse	#
Ps 66:20	Blessed be God, which hath not turned away my prayer, nor his mercy from me.	8605
Ps 69:13	But as for me, my prayer is unto thee, O LORD, in an acceptable time: O God, in the multitude of thy mercy hear me, in the truth of thy salvation.	8605
Ps 72:15	And he shall live, and to him shall be given of the gold of Sheba: prayer also shall be made for him continually; and daily shall he be praised.	6419
Ps 80:4	O LORD God of hosts, how long wilt thou be angry against the prayer of thy people?	8605
Ps 84:8	O LORD God of hosts, hear my prayer: give ear, O God of Jacob. Selah.	8605
Ps 86:6	Give ear, O LORD, unto my prayer; and attend to the voice of my supplications.	8605
Ps 88:13	But unto thee have I cried, O LORD; and in the morning shall my prayer prevent thee.	8605

by Dr. Ralph Stowe   186

From Your Lips To God's Ear

Verse	Text of verse	#
Ps 88:2	Let my prayer come before thee: incline thine ear unto my cry;	8 6 0 5
Rom 8:26	Likewise the Spirit also helpeth our infirmities: for we know not what we should pray for as we ought: but the Spirit itself maketh intercession for us with groanings which cannot be uttered.	4 3 3 6
Rom 10:1	Brethren, my heart's desire and prayer to God for Israel is, that they might be saved.	1 1 6 2
Rom 12:12	Rejoicing in hope; patient in tribulation; continuing instant in prayer;	4 3 3 5
Ruth 2:7	And she said, I pray you, let me glean and gather after the reapers among the sheaves: so she came, and hath continued even from the morning until now, that she tarried a little in the house.	4 9 9 4
Zech 7:2	When they had sent unto the house of God Sherezer and Regemmelech, and their men, to pray before the LORD,	2 4 7 0
Zech 8:21	And the inhabitants of one city shall go to another, saying, Let us go speedily to pray before the LORD, and to seek the LORD of hosts: I will go also.	2 4 7 0

by Dr. Ralph Stowe

Verse	Text of verse	#
Zech 8:22	Yea, many people and strong nations shall come to seek the LORD of hosts in Jerusalem, and to pray before the LORD.	3 4 7 0

Appendix II: Strong's definitions

Professor of Exegetical Theology at Drew Theological Seminary, Dr. James Strong published his monumental concordance to the Holy Scriptures in 1890. Labor by Dr. Strong and more than 100 colleagues over a 35 year period resulted in his widely used concordance which was compiled from the King James Version of the Bible. This was done without the aid of computers or other electronic devices. Strong's has stood the test of time and has confirmed Professor Strong's efforts to offer a complete, simple, and accurate concordance. As the General Preface to the 1890 Edition stated, it is "a permanent standard for purposes of reference."

For those unfamiliar with the work, it has listed each word used in the 'original' work that was translated into the King James Bible and assigned to each word a number.

by Dr. Ralph Stowe   188

From Your Lips To God's Ear

Listing the number, the word used, definition most believed to be in use at the 'original' writing, and the etymology of the 'original' word, i.e., reference of from which the word came, it offers the student an understanding of the flavor of the intent of how words were meant to be interpreted.

It is not the purpose of this appendix to reproduce Strong's work. The reader can find 'improved' versions being offered by various publishers. Each claiming to add a benefit to the original work, the student is encouraged to investigate this and other tools best fitting their need. The limited information relative to the Strong's numbers for the words translated as 'pray' in the verses from Appendix I are presented in the table below for convenience of the reader while studying this book.

Hebrew or Greek Word Translated	Word Derivation
577 'anna' (awn-naw');	160 'ahabah (a-hab-aw);
or 'annah (awn-naw'); apparent contracted from 160 and 4994; oh now!:	feminine of 158 and meaning the same:
KJV-- I (me) beseech **(pray)** thee, O. ***. 'anah. See 576, ***. 'anah. See 575.	KJV-- love.
	158 'ahab (ah'-hab);

From Your Lips To God's Ear

Hebrew or Greek Word Translated	Word Derivation

from 157; affection (in a good or a bad sense):

KJV-- love (-r).

157 'ahab (aw-hab');

or 'aheb (aw-habe'); a primitive root; to have affection for (sexually or otherwise):

KJV-- (be-) love (-d, -ly, -r), like, friend.

1156 daneion (dan'-i-on);	1325 didomi (did'-o-mee);

from danos (a gift); probably akin to the base of 1325; a loan:

KJV-- debt.

a prolonged form of a primary verb (which is used as an altern. in most of the tenses); to give (used in a very wide application, properly, or by implication, literally or figuratively; greatly modified by the connection):

KJV-- adventure, bestow, bring forth, commit, deliver (up), give, grant, hinder, make, minister, number, offer, have power, put, receive, set, shew, smite (+with the hand), strike (+with the palm of the hand), suffer, take, utter, yield.

From Your Lips To God's Ear

2470 chalah (khaw-law');

a primitive root [compare 2342, 2470, 2490];
properly, to be rubbed or worn; hence
(figuratively) to be weak, sick, afflicted; or
(causatively) to grieve, make sick; also to stroke
(in flattering), entreat:

KJV-- beseech, (be) diseased, (put to) grief, be
grieved, (be) grievous, infirmity, intreat, lay to,
put to pain, X **pray**, make **pray**er, be (fall,
make) sick, sore, be sorry, make suit (X
supplication), woman in travail, be (become)
weak, be wounded.

2603 chanan (khaw-nan');

a primitive root [compare 2583]; properly, to
bend or stoop in kindness to an inferior; to
favor, bestow; causatively to implore (i.e. move
to favor by petition):

KJV-- beseech, X fair, (be, find, shew) favour (-
able), be (deal, give, grant (gracious (-ly),
intreat, (be) merciful, have (shew) mercy (on,
upon), have pity upon, **pray**, make supplication,
X very.

3863 luw' (loo);

or lu' (loo); or luw (loo); a conditional particle;
if; by implication (interj. as a wish) would that!:

KJV-- if (haply), peradventure, I **pray** thee,
though, I would, would God (that).

4994 na' (naw);

by Dr. Ralph Stowe   191

a primitive particle of incitement and entreaty, which may usually be rendered: "I **pray**," "now," or "then"; added mostly to verbs (in the Imperative or Future), or to interjections, occasionally to an adverb or conjunction:

KJV-- I beseech (**pray**) thee (you), go to, now, oh.

6279 `athar (aw-thar');

a primitive root [rather denominative from 6281]; to burn incense in worship, i.e. intercede (reciprocally, listen to **pray**er):

KJV-- intreat, (make) **pray** (-er).

6281 `Ether (eh'ther);

from 6280; abundance; Ether, a place in Palestine:

KJV-- Ether.

6280 `athar (aw-thar');

a primitive root; to be (causatively, make) abundant:

KJV-- deceitful, multiply.

6293 paga` (paw-gah');

a primitive root; to impinge, by accident or violence, or (figuratively) by importunity:

KJV-- come (betwixt), cause to entreat, fall (upon), make intercession, intercessor, intreat, lay, light [upon], meet (together), **pray**, reach, run.

6419 palal (paw-lal');

a primitive root; to judge (officially or

by Dr. Ralph Stowe   192

mentally); by extension, to intercede, **pray**:

KJV-- intreat, judge (-ment), (make) **pray** (-er, -ing), make supplication.

6739 tsela' (Aramaic) (tsel-aw');probably corresponding to 6760 in the sense of bowing; pray: KJV-- **pray**.

6760 tsala`** (tsaw-lah');a primitive root: probably to curve; used only as denominative from 6763, to limp (as if one-sided): KJV-- halt.**6763 tsela` (tsay-law');or (feminine) tsal`ah (tsal-aw'); from 6760; a rib (as curved), literally (of the body) or figuratively (of a door, i.e. leaf); hence, a side, literally (of a person) or figuratively (of an object or the sky, i.e. quarter); architecturally, a (especially floor or ceiling) timber or plank (single or collective, i.e. a flooring): KJV-- beam, board, chamber, corner, leaf, plank, rib, side (chamber).

7592 sha'al (shaw-al');

or sha'el (shaw-ale'); a primitive root; to inquire; by implication, to request; by extension, to demand:

KJV-- ask (counsel, on), beg, borrow, lay to charge, consult, demand, desire, X earnestly, enquire, + greet, obtain leave, lend, **pray**, request, require, + salute, X straitly, X surely, wish.

7878 siyach (see'-akh);

a primitive root; to ponder, i.e. (by implication) converse (with oneself, and hence, aloud) or (transitively) utter:

KJV-- commune, complain, declare, meditate, muse, **pray**, speak, talk (with).

7879 siyach (see'-akh);

from 7878; a contemplation; by implication, an utterance:

KJV-- babbling, communication, complaint, meditation, **pray**er, talk.

7881 siychah (see-khaw');

feminine of 7879; reflection; be extension, devotion:

KJV-- meditation, **pray**er.

8605 tephillah (tef-il-law');

from 6419; intercession, supplication; by implication, a hymn:

KJV-- **pray**er.

6419 palal (paw-lal');

a primitive root; to judge (officially or mentally); by extension, to intercede, **pray**:

KJV-- intreat, judge (-ment), (make) **pray** (-er, -ing), make supplication.

From Your Lips To God's Ear

Hebrew or Greek Word Translated	Word Derivation

1162 deesis (deh'-ay-sis);

from 1189; a petition:

KJV-- **pray**er, request, supplication.

1183 dekatoo (dek-at-o'-o);	**1181 dekate (dek-at'-ay);**
from 1181; to tithe, i.e. to give or take a tenth:	feminine of 1182; a tenth, i.e. as a percentage or (tech.) tithe:
KJV-- pay (receive) tithes.	
	KJV-- tenth (part), tithe.
1189 deomai (deh'-om-ahee);	**1210 deo (deh'-o);**
middle voice of 1210; to beg (as binding oneself), i.e. petition:	a primary verb; to bind (in various applications, literally or figuratively):
KJV-- beseech, **pray** (to), make request. Compare 4441. ***. deon. See 1163.	KJV-- bind, be in bonds, knit, tie, wind. See also 1163, 1189.
2065 erotao (er-o-tah'-o);	**2046 ereo (er-eh'-o);**
apparently from 2046 [compare 2045]; to interrogate; by implication, to request:	probably a fuller form of 4483; an alternate for 2036 in cert. tenses; to utter, i.e. speak or say:
KJV-- ask, beseech, desire, intreat, **pray**. Compare 4441.	KJV-- call, say, speak (of), tell.
	4483 rheo (hreh'-o);
	for certain tenses of which a prolonged form

by Dr. Ralph Stowe

From Your Lips To God's Ear

ereo (er-eh'-o); is used; and both as alternate for 2036; perhaps akin (or ident.) with 4482 (through the idea of pouring forth); to utter, i.e. speak or say:

KJV-- command, make, say, speak (of). Compare 3004.

2171 euche (yoo-khay');

from 2172; properly, a wish, expressed as a petition to God, or in votive obligation:

KJV-- **pray**er, vow.

2172 euchomai (yoo'-khom-ahee);middle voice of a primary verb; to wish; by implication, to **pray** to God: KJV-- **pray**, will, wish.

3870 parakaleo (par-ak-al-eh'-o);

from 3844 and 2564; to call near, i.e. invite, invoke (by imploration, hortation or consolation):

KJV-- beseech, call for, (be of good) comfort, desire, (give) exhort (-ation), intreat, **pray**.

3844 para (par-ah');

a primary preposition; properly, near; i.e. (with genitive case) from beside (literally or figuratively), (with dative case) at (or in) the vicinity of (objectively or subjectively), (with accusative case) to the proximity with (local [especially beyond or opposed to] or causal [on account of]:

From Your Lips To God's Ear

KJV-- above, against, among, at, before, by, contrary to, X friend, from, + give [such things as they], + that [she] had, X his, in, more than, nigh unto, (out) of, past, save, side ... by, in the sight of, than, [therefore-], with. In compounds it retains the same variety of application.

4335 proseuche (pros-yoo-khay');

from 4336; **pray**er (worship); by implication, an oratory (chapel):

KJV-- X **pray** earnestly, **prayer.**

4336 proseuchomai (pros-yoo'-khom-ahee);

from 4314 and 2172; to **pray** to God, i.e. supplicate, worship:

KJV-- **pray** (X earnestly, for), make **prayer.**

4314 pros (pros);

a strengthened form of 4253; a preposition of direction; forward to, i.e. toward (with the genitive case the side of, i.e. pertaining to; with the dative case by the side of, i.e. near to; usually with the accusative case the place, time, occasion, or respect, which is the destination of the relation, i.e. whither or for which it is predicated):

From Your Lips To God's Ear

Hebrew or Greek Word Translated	Word Derivation

KJV-- about, according to against, among, at, because of, before, between, ([where-]) by, for, X at thy house, in, for intent, nigh unto, of, which pertain to, that, to (the end that), X together, to ([you]) - ward, unto, with (-in). In comparison it denotes essentially the same applications, namely, motion towards, accession to, or nearness at.

4253 pro (pro);

a primary preposition; "fore", i.e. in front of, prior (figuratively, superior) to:

KJV-- above, ago, before, or ever. In comparison it retains the same significations.

by Dr. Ralph Stowe

Appendix III: Key Words In Context

Below in the right column is an alphabetical listing of 'pray' and the characters that follow it at each occurrence in a verse. This can be useful in finding a desired verse or topic. It is presented here for the convenience of the reader in verifying the text. For each use listed, the center column presents the words preceding the listing. The left column refers the reader to the original verse in the scriptures where the word is found.

Verse	Text leading 'pray'	Text following 'pray'
Acts 10:9	went up upon the housetop to	**pray** about the sixth hour:
2 Th 1:11	Wherefore also we	**pray** always for you, that our God would count you worthy
Luke 21:36	Watch ye therefore, and	**pray** always, that ye may be accounted worthy to escape
2 Chr 6:24	and confess thy name, and	**pray** and make supplication before thee in this house;
Zech 7:2	, and their men, to	**pray** before the LORD,
Zech 8:21	, saying, Let us go speedily to	**pray** before the LORD, and to seek the LORD of hosts: I will go also.
Zech 8:22	of hosts in Jerusalem, and to	**pray** before the LORD.

From Your Lips To God's Ear

Verse	Text leading 'pray'	Text following 'pray'
Neh 1:6	**pray**er of thy servant, which I	**pray** before thee now, day and night, for the children of
1 Chr 17:25	hath found in his heart to	**pray** before thee.
1 Tim 2:8	I will therefore that men	**pray** every where, lifting up holy hands, without wrath and doubting.
Rom 8:26	or we know not what we should	**pray** for as we ought: but the Spirit itself maketh intercession for us with
1 John 5:16	death: I do not say that he shall	**pray** for it.
1 Kings 13:6	face of the LORD thy God, and	**pray** for me, that my hand may be restored me again.
Ezra 6:10	unto the God of heaven, and	**pray** for the life of the king, and of his sons.
Ps 122:6		**Pray** for the peace of Jerusalem: they shall prosper that love thee.
Gen 20:7	for he is a prophet, and he shall	**pray** for thee, and thou shalt live: and if thou restore her.
Matt 5:44	to them that hate you, and	**pray** for them which despitefully use you, and persecute you;
Luke 6:28	Bless them that curse you, and	**pray** for them which despitefully use you.
John 17:9	I	**pray** for them: I **pray** not for the world, but for them which thou hast
1 Sam 12:19	all the people said unto Samuel,	**Pray** for thy servants unto the LORD thy God, that we die not: for

by Dr. Ralph Stowe

From Your Lips To God's Ear

Verse	Text leading 'pray'	Text following 'pray'
Jer 42:20	the LORD your God, saying,	**Pray** for us unto the LORD our God; and according unto
Jer 42:2	be accepted before thee, and	**pray** for us unto the LORD thy God, even for all this
2 Th 3:1	Finally, brethren,	**pray** for us, that the word of the Lord may have free course, and be
1 Thes 5:25	Brethren,	**pray** for us.
Heb 13:18		**Pray** for us: for we trust we have a good conscience, in all things willing
1 Sam 7:5	all Israel to Mizpeh, and I will	**pray** for you unto the LORD.
Col 1:9	we heard it, do not cease to	**pray** for you, and to desire that ye might be filled with the
1 Sam 12:23	against the LORD in ceasing to	**pray** for you: but I will teach you the good and the right way:
Job 42:8	; and my servant Job shall	**pray** for you: for him will I accept: lest I deal with you
2 Tim 4:16	me, but all men forsook me: I	**pray** God that it may not be laid to their charge.
1 Thes 5:23	peace sanctify you wholly; and I	**pray** God your whole spirit and soul and body be preserved blameless
Acts 8:22	of this thy wickedness, and	**pray** God, if perhaps the thought of thine heart may be forgiven thee.
Mark 5:17	And they began to	**pray** him to depart out of their coasts.

by Dr. Ralph Stowe

From Your Lips To God's Ear

Verse	Text leading 'pray'	Text following 'pray'
John 17:20	Neither	**pray** I for these alone, but for them also which shall believe on me
1 Cor 14:14	For if I	**pray** in an unknown tongue, my spirit prayeth, but my understanding
2 Chr 6:32	out arm; if they come and	**pray** in this house;
John 17:9	I **pray** for them: I	**pray** not for the world, but for them which thou hast given me; for they
Jer 14:11	Then said the LORD unto me,	**Pray** not for this people for their good.
John 17:15	I	**pray** not that thou shouldest take them out of the world, but that thou
Jer 11:14	Therefore	**pray** not thou for this people, neither lift up a cry or prayer
Jer 7:16	Therefore	**pray** not thou for this people, neither lift up cry nor **pray**er
Jer 37:3	the prophet Jeremiah, saying,	**Pray** now unto the LORD our God for us.
Jer 37:3	the prophet Jeremiah, saying,	**Pray** now unto the LORD our God for us.
Judg 9:38	thou hast despised? go out, I	**pray** now, and fight with them.
James 5:16	your faults one to another, and	**pray** one for another, that ye may be healed. The effectual fervent
James 5:14	of the church; and let them	**pray** over him, anointing him with oil in the name of the Lord:

by Dr. Ralph Stowe   202

From Your Lips To God's Ear

Verse	Text leading 'pray'	Text following 'pray'
Matt 6:5	hypocrites are: for they love to	**pray** standing in the synagogues and in the corners of the streets,
1 Cor 14:13	speaketh in an unknown tongue	**pray** that he may interpret.
1 Cor 14:13	speaketh in an unknown tongue	**pray** that he may interpret.
Luke 22:40	at the place, he said unto them,	**Pray** that ye enter not into temptation.
John 16:26	I say not unto you, that I will	**pray** the Father for you:
John 14:16	And I will	**pray** the Father, and he shall give you another Comforter, that he may
Luke 14:18	I must needs go and see it: I	**pray** thee have me excused.
Luke 14:19	oxen, and I go to prove them: I	**pray** thee have me excused.
1 Sam 3:17	LORD hath said unto thee? I	**pray** thee hide it not from me: God do so to thee, and more also, if thou
Gen 50:17	ye say unto Joseph, Forgive, I	**pray** thee now, the trespass of thy brethren, and their sin; for they did
Acts 24:4	not further tedious unto thee, I	**pray** thee that thou wouldest hear us of thy clemency a few words.
Luke 16:27	Then he said, I	**pray** thee therefore, father, that thou wouldest send him to my
1 Kings 17:10	to her, and said, Fetch me, I	**pray** thee, a little water in a vessel, that I may drink.

by Dr. Ralph Stowe   203

From Your Lips To God's Ear

Verse	Text leading 'pray'	Text following 'pray'
Gen 24:43	, and I say to her, Give me, I	**pray** thee, a little water of thy pitcher to drink;
Judg 4:19	And he said unto her, Give me, I	**pray** thee, a little water to drink; for I am thirsty. And she
1 Kings 17:11	to her, and said, Bring me, I	**pray** thee, a morsel of bread in thine hand.
2 Kings 5:22	of the prophets: give them, I	**pray** thee, a talent of silver, and two changes of garments.
2 Kings 8:4	man of God, saying, Tell me, I	**pray** thee, all the great things that Elisha hath done.
2 Sam 18:22	Joab, But howsoever, let me, I	**pray** thee, also run after Cushi. And Joab said, Wherefore wilt thou run,
Gen 50:5	, Now therefore let me go up, I	**pray** thee, and bury my father, and I will come again.
1 Kings 14:2	said to his wife, Arise, I	**pray** thee, and disguise thyself, that thou be not
Judg 13:4	Now therefore beware, I	**pray** thee, and drink not wine nor strong drink, and eat not any
2 Kings 6:3	And one said, Be content, I	**pray** thee, and go with thy servants. And he answered, I will go.
Jer 40:15	secretly, saying, Let me go, I	**pray** thee, and I will slay Ishmael the son of Nethaniah,
Judg 19:11	said unto his master, Come, I	**pray** thee, and let us turn in into this city of the Jebusites, and lodge in it.
Exod 4:18	and said unto him, Let me go, I	**pray** thee, and return unto my brethren which are in Egypt, and see

by Dr. Ralph Stowe   204

From Your Lips To God's Ear

Verse	Text leading 'pray'	Text following 'pray'
1 Sam 20:29	in thine eyes, let me get away, I	**pray** thee, and see my brethren. Therefore he cometh not unto the
2 Kings 2:16	strong men; let them go, we	**pray** thee, and seek thy master: lest peradventure the Spirit of the LORD
Judg 16:28	, O Lord GOD, remember me, I	**pray** thee, and strengthen me, I **pray** thee, only this
2 Sam 16:9	lord the king? let me go over, I	**pray** thee, and take off his head.
Judg 19:6	unto the man, Be content, I	**pray** thee, and tarry all night, and let thine heart be merry.
2 Chr 18:4	unto the king of Israel, Inquire, I	**pray** thee, at the word of the LORD to day.
1 Kings 22:5	unto the king of Israel, Inquire, I	**pray** thee, at the word of the LORD to day.
Jer 37:20	the king: let my supplication, I	**pray** thee, be accepted before thee; that thou cause me not
2 Sam 24:17	they done? let thine hand, I	**pray** thee, be against me, and against my father's house.
2 Kings 5:17	said, Shall there not then, I	**pray** thee, be given to thy servant two mules' burden of
2 Chr 18:12	assent; let thy word therefore, I	**pray** thee, be like one of theirs, and speak thou good.
1 Kings 22:13	with one mouth: let thy word, I	**pray** thee, be like the word of one of them, and speak that which is good.
1 Kings 8:26	, O God of Israel, let thy word, I	**pray** thee, be verified, which thou spakest unto thy servant David my
1 Sam 15:30	sinned: yet honour me now, I	**pray** thee, before the elders of my people, and before Israel, and turn

by Dr. Ralph Stowe   205

From Your Lips To God's Ear

Verse	Text leading 'pray'	Text following 'pray'
Gen 13:8	Lot, Let there be no strife, I	**pray** thee, between me and thee, and between my herdmen and thy
1 Sam 30:7	the priest, Ahimelech's son, I	**pray** thee, bring me hither the ephod. And Abiathar brought thither
Judg 6:39	but this once: let me prove, I	**pray** thee, but this once with the fleece; let it now be dry only upon
Exod 4:13	And he said, O my Lord, send, I	**pray** thee, by the hand of him whom thou wilt send.
Mark 5:23	lieth at the point of death: I	**pray** thee, come and lay thy hands on her, that she may be healed; and
1 Sam 22:3	Let my father and my mother, I	**pray** thee, come forth, and be with you, till I know what God will do for
Num 22:17	unto me: come therefore, I	**pray** thee, curse me this people.
Num 22:6	Come now therefore, I	**pray** thee, curse me this people; for they are too mighty for me:
1 Sam 28:8	woman by night: and he said, I	**pray** thee, divine unto me by the familiar spirit, and bring me him up,
Gen 24:17	to meet her, and said, Let me, I	**pray** thee, drink a little water of thy pitcher.
2 Sam 14:2	woman, and said unto her, I	**pray** thee, feign thyself to be a mourner, and put on now mourning
2 Kings 7:13	and said, Let some take, I	**pray** thee, five of the horses that remain, which are left in the city,

by Dr. Ralph Stowe

From Your Lips To God's Ear

Verse	Text leading 'pray'	Text following 'pray'
Jonah 1:8	said they unto him, Tell us, we	**pray** thee, for whose cause this evil is upon us; What is thine
Gen 50:17	did unto thee evil: and now, we	**pray** thee, forgive the trespass of the servants of the
1 Sam 25:28	I	**pray** thee, forgive the trespass of thine handmaid: for the LORD will
Gen 13:9	before thee? separate thyself, I	**pray** thee, from me: if thou wilt take the left hand, then I will go to the
Gen 32:11	Deliver me, I	**pray** thee, from the hand of my brother, from the hand of
Gen 18:3	in thy sight, pass not away, I	**pray** thee, from thy servant:
2 Kings 18:23	Now therefore, I	**pray** thee, give pledges to my lord the king of Assyria, and I
1 Kings 1:12	Now therefore come, let me, I	**pray** thee, give thee counsel, that thou mayest save thine own life, and
Josh 7:19	said unto Achan, My son, give, I	**pray** thee, glory to the LORD God of Israel, and make
Exod 34:9	thy sight, O Lord, let my Lord, I	**pray** thee, go among us; for it is a stiffnecked people; and pardon our
Gen 16:2	restrained me from bearing: I	**pray** thee, go in unto my maid; it may be that I may obtain children
Gen 23:13	, saying, But if thou wilt give it, I	**pray** thee, hear me: I will give thee money for the field; take
Job 33:1	Wherefore, Job, I	**pray** thee, hear my speeches, and hearken to all my words.

by Dr. Ralph Stowe

From Your Lips To God's Ear

Verse	Text leading 'pray'	Text following 'pray'
1 Sam 28:22	Now therefore, I	**pray** thee, hearken thou also unto the voice of thine handmaid, and let
2 Kings 2:6	And Elijah said unto him, Tarry, I	**pray** thee, here; for the LORD hath sent me to Jordan. And
Num 22:16	the son of Zippor, Let nothing, I	**pray** thee, hinder thee from coming unto me:
Num 23:27	Balak said unto Balaam, Come, I	**pray** thee, I will bring thee unto another place;
Gen 30:27	And Laban said unto him, I	**pray** thee, if I have found favour in thine eyes, tarry: for
Exod 33:13	Now therefore, I	**pray** thee, if I have found grace in thy sight, shew me now thy way,
Gen 33:10	And Jacob said, Nay, I	**pray** thee, if now I have found grace in thy sight, then receive
Gen 47:29	truly with me; bury me not, I	**pray** thee, in Egypt:
Judg 15:2	sister fairer than she? take her, I	**pray** thee, instead of her.
1 Sam 2:36	bread, and shall say, Put me, I	**pray** thee, into one of the priests' offices, that I may eat a piece of
1 Kings 19:20	after Elijah, and said, Let me, I	**pray** thee, kiss my father and my mother, and then I will
2 Kings 2:9	from thee. And Elisha said, I	**pray** thee, let a double portion of thy spirit be upon me.
Gen 38:16	by the way, and said, Go to, I	**pray** thee, let me come in unto thee; (for he knew not that she was

by Dr. Ralph Stowe

From Your Lips To God's Ear

Verse	Text leading 'pray'	Text following 'pray'
2 Sam 15:7	at Absalom said unto the king, I	**pray** thee, let me go and pay my vow, which I have vowed unto the
Deut 3:25	I	**pray** thee, let me go over, and see the good land that is beyond
1 Kings 20:32	Thy servant Ben-ha'dad saith, I	**pray** thee, let me live. And he said, Is he yet alive? he is my brother.
2 Sam 13:26	Then said Absalom, If not, I	**pray** thee, let my brother Amnon go with us. And the king said unto
2 Kings 1:13	said unto him, O man of God, I	**pray** thee, let my life, and the life of these fifty thy servants, be precious
1 Sam 26:19	Now therefore, I	**pray** thee, let my lord the king hear the words of his servant. If the
2 Sam 13:5	to see thee, say unto him, I	**pray** thee, let my sister Tamar come, and give me meat, and dress
2 Sam 13:6	, Amnon said unto the king, I	**pray** thee, let Tamar my sister come, and make me a couple of
2 Sam 14:11	Then said she, I	**pray** thee, let the king remember the LORD thy God,
1 Kings 17:21	, and said, O LORD my God, I	**pray** thee, let this child's soul come into him again.
Gen 44:33	Now therefore, I	**pray** thee, let thy servant abide instead of the lad a bondman to my
Gen 47:4	of Canaan: now therefore, we	**pray** thee, let thy servants dwell in the land of Goshen.

by Dr. Ralph Stowe

From Your Lips To God's Ear

Verse	Text leading 'pray'	Text following 'pray'
Judg 13:15	unto the angel of the LORD, I	**pray** thee, let us detain thee, until we shall have made ready a kid for
Gen 33:11	Take, I	**pray** thee, my blessing that is brought to thee; because God
Exod 10:17	Now therefore forgive, I	**pray** thee, my sin only this once, and intreat the LORD your God, that
1 Chr 21:17	they done? let thine hand, I	**pray** thee, O LORD my God, be on me, and on my father's
Jonah 4:2	unto the LORD, and said, I	**pray** thee, O LORD, was not this my saying, when I was yet
Jer 37:20	Therefore hear now, I	**pray** thee, O my lord the king: let my supplication, I **pray**
Judg 18:5	said unto him, Ask counsel, we	**pray** thee, of God, that we may know whether our way which we go
Job 8:8	For inquire, I	**pray** thee, of the former age, and prepare thyself to the search of their
Jer 21:2	Inquire, I	**pray** thee, of the LORD for us; for Nebuchadrezzar king of
Gen 30:14	Rachel said to Leah, Give me, I	**pray** thee, of thy son's mandrakes.
Acts 8:34	answered Philip, and said, I	**pray** thee, of whom speaketh the prophet this? of himself, or of some
2 Kings 4:10	Let us make a little chamber, I	**pray** thee, on the wall; and let us set for him there a bed, and a table, and
2 Kings 4:22	husband, and said, Send me, I	**pray** thee, one of the young men, and one of the asses, that I may run

From Your Lips To God's Ear

Verse	Text leading 'pray'	Text following 'pray'
Judg 16:28	thee, and strengthen me, I	**pray** thee, only this once, O God, that I may be at once avenged of
2 Kings 6:17	Elisha **pray**ed, and said, LORD, I	**pray** thee, open his eyes, that he may see. And the LORD
Num 11:15	thou deal thus with me, kill me, I	**pray** thee, out of hand, if I have found favour in thy
Exod 32:32	their sin--; and if not, blot me, I	**pray** thee, out of thy book which thou hast written.
1 Sam 15:25	Now therefore, I	**pray** thee, pardon my sin, and turn again with me, that I may worship
Gen 33:14	Let my lord, I	**pray** thee, pass over before his servant: and I will lead on
Judg 11:17	king of Edom, saying, Let me, I	**pray** thee, pass through thy land: but the king of Edom
1 Kings 20:31	Israel are merciful kings: let us, I	**pray** thee, put sackcloth on our loins, and ropes upon our heads,
1 Sam 25:25	Let not my lord, I	**pray** thee, regard this man of Belial, even Nabal: for as his name is, so is
1 Kings 2:20	one small petition of thee; I	**pray** thee, say me not nay. And the king said unto her, Ask
Gen 37:14	And he said to him, Go, I	**pray** thee, see whether it be well with thy brethren, and well
Gen 24:12	God of my master Abraham, I	**pray** thee, send me good speed this day, and shew
Gen 27:19	as thou badest me: arise, I	**pray** thee, sit and eat of my venison, that thy soul may bless me.

by Dr. Ralph Stowe   211

From Your Lips To God's Ear

Verse	Text leading 'pray'	Text following 'pray'
Gen 44:18	, Oh my lord, let thy servant, I	**pray** thee, speak a word in my lord's ears, and let not thine anger burn
1 Sam 25:24	be: and let thine handmaid, I	**pray** thee, speak in thine audience, and hear the words of thine
2 Sam 14:12	said, Let thine handmaid, I	**pray** thee, speak one word unto my lord the king. And he said, Say on.
2 Sam 13:13	fools in Israel. Now therefore, I	**pray** thee, speak unto the king; for he will not withhold me from thee.
1 Sam 16:22	to Jesse, saying, Let David, I	**pray** thee, stand before me; for he hath found favour in my sight.
2 Kings 5:15	, but in Israel: now therefore, I	**pray** thee, take a blessing of thy servant.
1 Sam 19:2	to kill thee: now therefore, I	**pray** thee, take heed to thyself until the morning, and abide in a secret
1 Sam 26:11	the LORD's anointed: but, I	**pray** thee, take thou now the spear that is at his bolster, and the cruse of
2 Sam 1:4	him, How went the matter? I	**pray** thee, tell me. And he answered, That the people are
Gen 24:14	shall say, Let down thy pitcher, I	**pray** thee, that I may drink; and she shall say, Drink, and I
Gen 27:21	said unto Jacob, Come near, I	**pray** thee, that I may feel thee, my son, whether thou be my very son
Jer 32:8	said unto me, Buy my field, I	**pray** thee, that is in Anathoth, which is in the country of

by Dr. Ralph Stowe

From Your Lips To God's Ear

Verse	Text leading 'pray'	Text following 'pray'
Judg 1:24	said unto him, Shew us, we	pray thee, the entrance into the city, and we will shew thee mercy.
Job 22:22	Receive, I	pray thee, the law from his mouth, and lay up his words in thine heart.
2 Kings 2:19	city said unto Elisha, Behold, I	pray thee, the situation of this city is pleasant, as my lord
2 Sam 14:18	the woman, Hide not from me, I	pray thee, the thing that I shall ask thee. And the woman said, Let my
Judg 10:15	unto thee; deliver us only, we	pray thee, this day.
Gen 12:13	Say, I	pray thee, thou art my sister: that it may be well with me for thy sake;
Exod 5:3	hath met with us: let us go, we	pray thee, three days' journey into the desert, and sacrifice unto the
Num 20:17	Let us pass, I	pray thee, through thy country: we will not pass through the fields, or
Judg 11:19	said unto him, Let us pass, we	pray thee, through thy land into my place.
Gen 47:29	found grace in thy sight, put, I	pray thee, thy hand under my thigh, and deal kindly and truly with
Gen 24:2	ruled over all that he had, Put, I	pray thee, thy hand under my thigh:
Ps 119:76	Let, I	pray thee, thy merciful kindness be for my comfort, according to thy
Gen 32:29	asked him, and said, Tell me, I	pray thee, thy name. And he said, Wherefore is it that thou

by Dr. Ralph Stowe   213

From Your Lips To God's Ear

Verse	Text leading 'pray'	Text following 'pray'
Neh 1:11	fear thy name: and prosper, I	**pray** thee, thy servant this day, and grant him mercy in
Gen 27:3	Now therefore take, I	**pray** thee, thy weapons, thy quiver and thy bow, and go out to the
2 Kings 4:26	Run now, I	**pray** thee, to meet her, and say unto her, Is it well with
Isa 36:8	Now therefore give pledges, I	**pray** thee, to my master the king of Assyria, and I will give
2 Kings 18:26	Joah, unto Rabshakeh, Speak, I	**pray** thee, to thy servants in the Syrian language; for we
2 Sam 19:37	Let thy servant, I	**pray** thee, turn back again, that I may die in mine own
2 Sam 15:31	. And David said, O LORD, I	**pray** thee, turn the counsel of Ahithophel into foolishness.
Judg 6:18	Depart not hence, I	**pray** thee, until I come unto thee, and bring forth my
2 Kings 6:2	Let us go, we	**pray** thee, unto Jordan, and take thence every man a
Gen 48:9	place. And he said, Bring them, I	**pray** thee, unto me, and I will bless them.
Gen 40:14	with thee, and shew kindness, I	**pray** thee, unto me, and make mention of me unto Pharaoh, and
1 Kings 2:17	And he said, Speak, I	**pray** thee, unto Solomon the king, (for he will not say thee
Isa 36:11	Joah unto Rabshakeh, Speak, I	**pray** thee, unto thy servants in the Syrian language; for we
2 Sam 1:9	He said unto me again, Stand, I	**pray** thee, upon me, and slay me: for anguish is come upon me,

by Dr. Ralph Stowe   214

From Your Lips To God's Ear

Verse	Text leading 'pray'	Text following 'pray'
1 Sam 10:15	And Saul's uncle said, Tell me, I	**pray** thee, what Samuel said unto you.
1 Sam 25:8	we come in a good day: give, I	**pray** thee, whatsoever cometh to thine hand unto thy servants, and
1 Sam 9:18	in the gate, and said, Tell me, I	**pray** thee, where the seer's house is.
Gen 37:16	, I seek my brethren: tell me, I	**pray** thee, where they feed their flocks.
Judg 16:6	Delilah said to Samson, Tell me, I	**pray** thee, wherein thy great strength lieth, and wherewith
Judg 16:10	, and told me lies: now tell me, I	**pray** thee, wherewith thou mightest be bound.
Job 4:7	Remember, I	**pray** thee, who ever perished, being innocent? or where were
Gen 38:25	child: and she said, Discern, I	**pray** thee, whose are these, the signet, and bracelets, and staff.
2 Kings 6:18	, and said, Smite this people, I	**pray** thee, with blindness. And he smote them with blindness
Num 23:13	Balak said unto him, Come, I	**pray** thee, with me unto another place, from whence
Gen 25:30	Esau said to Jacob, Feed me, I	**pray** thee, with that same red pottage; for I am faint: therefore
1 Sam 26:8	therefore let me smite him, I	**pray** thee, with the spear even to the earth at once, and I will not
Gen 24:45	I said unto her, Let me drink, I	**pray** thee.
1 Kings 20:35	word of the LORD, Smite me, I	**pray** thee. And the man refused to smite him.

by Dr. Ralph Stowe   215

From Your Lips To God's Ear

Verse	Text leading 'pray'	Text following 'pray'
1 Kings 20:37	man, and said, Smite me, I	**pray** thee. And the man smote him, so that in smiting he wounded him.
Judg 19:8	said, Comfort thine heart, I	**pray** thee. And they tarried until afternoon, and they did eat both of
Isa 29:12	not learned, saying, Read this, I	**pray** thee: and he saith, I am not learned.
Isa 29:11	at is learned, saying, Read this, I	**pray** thee: and he saith, I cannot; for it is sealed:
Gen 24:23	daughter art thou? tell me, I	**pray** thee: is there room in thy father's house for us to lodge in?
1 Sam 20:29	And he said, Let me go, I	**pray** thee; for our family hath a sacrifice in the city; and my brother,
2 Kings 2:2	said unto Elisha, Tarry here, I	**pray** thee; for the LORD hath sent me to Bethel. And Elisha
2 Kings 2:4	unto him, Elisha, tarry here, I	**pray** thee; for the LORD hath sent me to Jericho. And he
Num 10:31	And he said, Leave us not, I	**pray** thee; forasmuch as thou knowest how we are to
2 Sam 7:27	servant found in his heart to	**pray** this **pray**er unto thee.
2 Cor 13:7	Now I	**pray** to God that ye do no evil; not that we should appear approved,
Matt 26:53	thou that I cannot now	**pray** to my Father, and he shall presently give me more than twelve
Matt 6:6	when thou hast shut thy door,	**pray** to thy Father which is in secret; and thy Father which

by Dr. Ralph Stowe   216

From Your Lips To God's Ear

Verse	Text leading 'pray'	Text following 'pray'
2 Chr 6:38	have carried them captives, and	**pray** toward their land, which thou gavest unto their fathers, and
1 Kings 8:42	arm;) when he shall come and	**pray** toward this house;
2 Chr 6:26	sinned against thee; yet if they	**pray** toward this place, and confess thy name, and turn from their sin,
1 Kings 8:35	sinned against thee; if they	**pray** toward this place, and confess thy name, and turn from their sin,
1 Kings 8:30	people Israel, when they shall	**pray** toward this place: and hear thou in heaven thy dwelling place:
Isa 45:20	of their graven image, and	**pray** unto a god that cannot save.
1 Cor 11:13	: is it comely that a woman	**pray** unto God uncovered?
1 Cor 11:13	: is it comely that a woman	**pray** unto God uncovered?
Job 33:26	He shall	**pray** unto God, and he will be favourable unto him: and he
Job 21:15	profit should we have, if we	**pray** unto him?
Jer 29:12	upon me, and ye shall go and	**pray** unto me, and I will hearken unto you.
Jer 29:7	be carried away captives, and	**pray** unto the LORD for it: for in the peace thereof shall ye have peace.
1 Kings 8:44	thou shalt send them, and shall	**pray** unto the LORD toward the city which thou hast chosen, and toward

From Your Lips To God's Ear

Verse	Text leading 'pray'	Text following 'pray'
Jer 42:4	have heard you; behold, I will	**pray** unto the LORD your God according to your words;
Num 21:7	the LORD, and against thee;	**pray** unto the LORD, that he take away the serpents from us. And
Ps 32:6	this shall every one that is godly	**pray** unto thee in a time when thou mayest be found: surely
2 Chr 6:37	carried captive, and turn and	**pray** unto thee in the land of their captivity, saying, We have sinned,
1 Kings 8:48	led them away captive, and	**pray** unto thee toward their land, which thou gavest unto
2 Chr 6:34	thou shalt send them, and they	**pray** unto thee toward this city which thou hast chosen, and the
1 Cor 14:15	What is it then? I will	**pray** with the spirit, and I will **pray** with the understanding also: I will
1 Cor 14:15	will **pray** with the spirit, and I will	**pray** with the understanding also: I will sing with the spirit, and I will sing
1Thes 5:17		**Pray** without ceasing.
Matt 24:20	But	**pray** ye that your flight be not in the winter, neither on the sabbath day:
Mark 13:18	And	**pray** ye that your flight be not in the winter.
Matt 9:38		**Pray** ye therefore the Lord of the harvest, that he will send
Luke 10:2	, but the labourers are few:	**pray** ye therefore the Lord of the harvest, that he would send forth

by Dr. Ralph Stowe

From Your Lips To God's Ear

Verse	Text leading 'pray'	Text following 'pray'
Acts 8:24	Then answered Simon, and said,	**Pray** ye to the Lord for me, that none of these things which ye have
Matt 6:9	After this manner therefore	**pray** ye: Our Father which art in heaven, Hallowed be thy name.
Matt 26:36	, Sit ye here, while I go and	**pray** yonder.
Gen 34:8	longeth for your daughter: I	**pray** you give her him to wife.
2 Cor 5:20	God did beseech you by us: we	**pray** you in Christ's stead, be ye reconciled to God.
Judg 19:9	day draweth toward evening, I	**pray** you tarry all night: behold, the day groweth to an
Acts 27:34	Wherefore I	**pray** you to take some meat: for this is for your health: for there shall
Job 32:21	Let me not, I	**pray** you, accept any man's person, neither let me give flattering titles
Lam 1:18	his commandment: hear, I	**pray** you, all people, and behold my sorrow: my virgins and my young
Ezek 33:30	to his brother, saying, Come, I	**pray** you, and hear what is the word that cometh forth from the
2 Kings 5:7	leprosy? wherefore consider, I	**pray** you, and see how he seeketh a quarrel against me.
1 Kings 20:7	of the land, and said, Mark, I	**pray** you, and see how this man seeketh mischief: for he sent unto
Gen 18:4	Let a little water, I	**pray** you, be fetched, and wash your feet, and rest yourselves under

by Dr. Ralph Stowe

From Your Lips To God's Ear

Verse	Text leading 'pray'	Text following 'pray'
Mal 1:9	And now, I	**pray** you, beseech God that he will be gracious unto us: this hath been
Isa 5:3	, and men of Judah, judge, I	**pray** you, betwixt me and my vineyard.
Gen 19:7	And said, I	**pray** you, brethren, do not so wickedly.
Gen 19:8	have not known man; let me, I	**pray** you, bring them out unto you, and do ye to them
Hag 2:15	And now, I	**pray** you, consider from this day and upward, from before a stone
Judg 19:23	them, Nay, my brethren, nay, I	**pray** you, do not so wickedly; seeing that this man is come into
Num 16:26	congregation, saying, Depart, I	**pray** you, from the tents of these wicked men, and touch nothing of
1 Sam 14:29	hath troubled the land: see, I	**pray** you, how mine eyes have been enlightened, because I tasted a
Judg 9:2	Speak, I	**pray** you, in the ears of all the men of Shechem, Whether is
Gen 50:4	grace in your eyes, speak, I	**pray** you, in the ears of Pharaoh, saying,
Gen 19:2	Behold now, my lords, turn in, I	**pray** you, into your servant's house, and tarry all night, and
Job 6:29	Return, I	**pray** you, let it not be iniquity; yea, return again, my righteousness is in
Ruth 2:7	she tarried a little in the house.	**pray** you, let me glean and gather after the reapers among the

by Dr. Ralph Stowe   220

From Your Lips To God's Ear

Verse	Text leading 'pray'	Text following 'pray'
Neh 5:10	of them money and corn: I	**pray** you, let us leave off this usury.
Judg 8:5	to the men of Succoth, Give, I	**pray** you, loaves of bread unto the people that follow me; for they be
Micah 3:1	And I said, Hear, I	**pray** you, O heads of Jacob, and ye princes of the house of
1 Sam 23:22	Go, I	**pray** you, prepare yet, and know and see his place where his haunt is,
Josh 2:12	Now therefore, I	**pray** you, swear unto me by the LORD, since I have
Num 22:19	Now therefore, I	**pray** you, tarry ye also here this night, that I may know what the
Gen 37:6	And he said unto them, Hear, I	**pray** you, this dream which I have dreamed:
Neh 5:11	Restore, I	**pray** you, to them, even this day, their lands, their
2 Sam 20:16	out of the city, Hear, hear; say, I	**pray** you, unto Joab, Come near hither, that I may speak with thee.
Micah 3:9	Hear this, I	**pray** you, ye heads of the house of Jacob, and princes of
Num 16:8	Moses said unto Korah, Hear, I	**pray** you, ye sons of Levi:
Gen 40:8	belong to God? tell me them, I	**pray** you.
Gen 45:4	brethren, Come near to me, I	**pray** you. And they came near. And he said, I am Joseph your brother,
Luke 6:12	he went out into a mountain to	**pray**, and continued all night in **pray**er to God.

by Dr. Ralph Stowe   221

From Your Lips To God's Ear

Verse	Text leading 'pray'	Text following 'pray'
Ps 55:17	and morning, and at noon, will I	**pray,** and cry aloud: and he shall hear my voice.
1 Kings 8:33	, and confess thy name, and	**pray,** and make supplication unto thee in this house:
Luke 18:1	end, that men ought always to	**pray,** and not to faint;
2 Chr 7:14	, shall humble themselves, and	**pray,** and seek my face, and turn from their wicked ways;
Luke 11:1	said unto him, Lord, teach us to	**pray,** as John also taught his disciples.
Luke 11:1	said unto him, Lord, teach us to	**pray,** as John also taught his disciples.
Mark 11:24	soever ye desire, when ye	**pray,** believe that ye receive them, and ye shall have them.
Luke 22:46	them, Why sleep ye? rise and	**pray,** lest ye enter into temptation.
Mark 14:38	Watch ye and	**pray,** lest ye enter into temptation. The spirit truly is ready, but the flesh
Luke 11:2	he said unto them, When ye	**pray,** say, Our Father which art in heaven, Hallowed be thy name. Thy
Matt 26:41	Watch and	**pray,** that ye enter not into temptation: the spirit indeed is
Phil 1:9	And this I	**pray,** that your love may abound yet more and more in knowledge
Matt 6:7	But when ye	**pray,** use not vain repetitions, as the heathen do: for they
Luke 9:28	and went up into a mountain to	**pray.**

by Dr. Ralph Stowe

From Your Lips To God's Ear

Verse	Text leading 'pray'	Text following 'pray'
Mark 14:32	disciples, Sit ye here, while I shall	**pray.**
Mark 6:46	he departed into a mountain to	**pray.**
Ps 5:2	and my God: for unto thee will I	**pray.**
James 5:13	among you afflicted? let him	**pray.** Is any merry? let him sing psalms.
Matt 19:13	put his hands on them, and	**pray:** and the disciples rebuked them.
Matt 14:23	up into a mountain apart to	**pray:** and when the evening was come, he was there alone.
Mark 13:33	Take ye heed, watch and	**pray:** for ye know not when the time is.
Isa 16:12	shall come to his sanctuary to	**pray;** but he shall not prevail.
Luke 18:10	men went up into the temple to	**pray;** the one a Pharisee, and the other a publican.
James 5:18	And he	**pray**ed again, and the heaven gave rain, and the earth brought forth her
2 Chr 32:20	prophet Isaiah the son of Amoz,	**pray**ed and cried to heaven.
Neh 1:4	certain days, and fasted, and	**pray**ed before the God of heaven,
2 Kings 19:15	And Hezekiah	**pray**ed before the LORD, and said, O LORD God of Israel,
James 5:17	like passions as we are, and he	**pray**ed earnestly that it might not rain: and it rained not on the earth

by Dr. Ralph Stowe

From Your Lips To God's Ear

Verse	Text leading 'pray'	Text following 'pray'
Deut 9:20	to have destroyed him: and I	**pray**ed for Aaron also the same time.
Job 42:10	the captivity of Job, when he	**pray**ed for his friends: also the LORD gave Job twice as much
Num 21:7	serpents from us. And Moses	**pray**ed for the people.
Luke 22:32	But I have	**pray**ed for thee, that thy faith fail not: and when thou art
2 Chr 30:18	it was written. But Hezekiah	**pray**ed for them, saying, The good LORD pardon every one
Acts 8:15	, when they were come down,	**pray**ed for them, that they might receive the Holy Ghost:
Mark 5:18	been possessed with the devil	**pray**ed him that he might be with him.
Luke 5:3	ships, which was Simon's, and	**pray**ed him that he would thrust out a little from the land. And he sat
Acts 16:9	stood a man of Macedonia, and	**pray**ed him, saying, Come over into Macedonia, and help us.
John 4:31	In the mean while his disciples	**pray**ed him, saying, Master, eat.
Acts 10:30	hour; and at the ninth hour I	**pray**ed in my house, and, behold, a man stood before me in bright
Acts 22:17	again to Jerusalem, even while I	**pray**ed in the temple, I was in a trance;
Acts 23:18	called me unto him, and	**pray**ed me to bring this young man unto thee, who hath something to
Luke 22:44	And being in an agony he	**pray**ed more earnestly: and his sweat was as it were great

by Dr. Ralph Stowe

From Your Lips To God's Ear

Verse	Text leading 'pray'	Text following 'pray'
Mark 14:35	little, and fell on the ground, and	**pray**ed that, if it were possible, the hour might pass from him.
Matt 26:44	, and went away again, and	**pray**ed the third time, saying the same words.
Deut 9:26	I	**pray**ed therefore unto the LORD, and said, O Lord GOD, destroy not
Acts 10:48	in the name of the Lord. Then	**pray**ed they him to tarry certain days.
Luke 18:11	The Pharisee stood and	**pray**ed thus with himself, God, I thank thee, that I am not as
Acts 10:2	much alms to the people, and	**pray**ed to God alway.
2 Kings 19:20	Israel, That which thou hast	**pray**ed to me against Sennacherib king of Assyria I have heard.
Isa 37:21	of Israel, Whereas thou hast	**pray**ed to me against Sennacherib king of Assyria:
Neh 2:4	dost thou make request? So I	**pray**ed to the God of heaven.
Gen 20:17	So Abraham	**pray**ed unto God: and God healed Abimelech, and his wife,
2 Chr 33:13	And	**pray**ed unto him: and he was intreated of him, and heard his
Jonah 2:1	Then Jonah	**pray**ed unto the LORD his God out of the fish's belly,
Dan 9:4	And I	**pray**ed unto the LORD my God, and made my confession, and said,

by Dr. Ralph Stowe   225

From Your Lips To God's Ear

Verse	Text leading 'pray'	Text following 'pray'
Isa 38:2	his face toward the wall, and	**pray**ed unto the LORD,
Jonah 4:2	And he	**pray**ed unto the LORD, and said, I **pray** thee, O LORD,
2 Kings 6:18	they came down to him, Elisha	**pray**ed unto the LORD, and said, Smite this people, I **pray**
1 Sam 1:10	was in bitterness of soul, and	**pray**ed unto the LORD, and wept sore.
2 Kings 20:2	turned his face to the wall, and	**pray**ed unto the LORD, saying,
Isa 37:15	And Hezekiah	**pray**ed unto the LORD, saying,
Jer 32:16	unto Baruch the son of Neriah, I	**pray**ed unto the LORD, saying,
Num 11:2	unto Moses; and when Moses	**pray**ed unto the LORD, the fire was quenched.
1 Sam 8:6	a king to judge us. And Samuel	**pray**ed unto the LORD.
2 Kings 4:33	the door upon them twain, and	**pray**ed unto the LORD.
2 Chr 32:24	was sick to the death, and	**pray**ed unto the LORD: and he spake unto him, and he gave him a
Acts 14:23	elders in every church, and had	**pray**ed with fasting, they commended them to the Lord, on
Acts 20:36	spoken, he kneeled down, and	**pray**ed with them all.
Luke 22:41	cast, and kneeled down, and	**pray**ed,

by Dr. Ralph Stowe   226

From Your Lips To God's Ear

Verse	Text leading 'pray'	Text following 'pray'
Dan 6:10	his knees three times a day, and	**pray**ed, and gave thanks before his God, as he did aforetime.
Acts 28:8	: to whom Paul entered in, and	**pray**ed, and laid his hands on him, and healed him.
Acts 13:3	And when they had fasted and	**pray**ed, and laid their hands on them, they sent them away.
1 Sam 2:1	And Hannah	**pray**ed, and said, My heart rejoiceth in the LORD, mine horn is exalted in
Acts 1:24	And they	**pray**ed, and said, Thou, Lord, which knowest the hearts of all men, shew
Acts 16:25	And at midnight Paul and Silas	**pray**ed, and sang praises unto God: and the prisoners heard them.
Mark 14:39	And again he went away, and	**pray**ed, and spake the same words.
Ezra 10:1	Now when Ezra had	**pray**ed, and when he had confessed, weeping and casting
Matt 26:39	further, and fell on his face, and	**pray**ed, saying, O my Father, if it be possible, let this cup pass from me:
Matt 26:42	again the second time, and	**pray**ed, saying, O my Father, if this cup may not pass away from me,
Luke 9:29	And as he	**pray**ed, the fashion of his countenance was altered, and
Acts 4:31	And when they had	**pray**ed, the place was shaken where they were assembled together; and
Acts 6:6	apostles: and when they had	**pray**ed, they laid their hands on them.

by Dr. Ralph Stowe

From Your Lips To God's Ear

Verse	Text leading 'pray'	Text following 'pray'
Acts 21:5	kneeled down on the shore, and	**pray**ed.
Luke 5:16	himself into the wilderness, and	**pray**ed.
Mark 1:35	into a solitary place, and there	**pray**ed.
1 Sam 1:27	For this child I	**pray**ed; and the LORD hath given me my petition which I asked of him:
Acts 9:40	all forth, and kneeled down, and	**pray**ed; and turning him to the body said, Tabitha, arise. And she
Ps 141:5	not break my head: for yet my	**pray**er also shall be in their calamities.
Ps 72:15	be given of the gold of Sheba:	**pray**er also shall be made for him continually; and daily shall he be
2 Chr 33:19	His	**pray**er also, and how God was intreated of him, and all his sin, and
Mark 9:29	come forth by nothing, but by	**pray**er and fasting.
Matt 17:21	this kind goeth not out but by	**pray**er and fasting.
Eph 6:18	**Pray**ing always with all	**pray**er and supplication in the Spirit, and watching thereunto with all
1 Kings 8:38	What	**pray**er and supplication soever be made by any man,
1 Kings 8:54	made an end of **pray**ing all this	**pray**er and supplication unto the LORD, he arose from

by Dr. Ralph Stowe

From Your Lips To God's Ear

Verse	Text leading 'pray'	Text following 'pray'
Phil 4:6	nothing; but in every thing by	**pray**er and supplication with thanksgiving let your requests be
Acts 1:14	all continued with one accord in	**pray**er and supplication, with the women, and Mary the mother of
Dan 9:3	unto the Lord God, to seek by	**pray**er and supplications, with fasting, and sackcloth, and ashes:
1 Kings 8:49	Then hear thou their	**pray**er and their supplication in heaven thy dwelling place, and
2 Chr 6:35	thou from the heavens their	**pray**er and their supplication, and maintain their cause.
1 Kings 8:45	Then hear thou in heaven their	**pray**er and their supplication, and maintain their cause.
2 Chr 6:39	from thy dwelling place, their	**pray**er and their supplications, and maintain their cause, and forgive thy
1 Kings 9:3	said unto him, I have heard thy	**pray**er and thy supplication, that thou hast made before
Ps 141:2	Let my	**pray**er be set forth before thee as incense; and the lifting up of my
Ps 109:7	him be condemned: and let his	**pray**er become sin.
Job 15:4	castest off fear, and restrainest	**pray**er before God.
Dan 9:13	upon us: yet made we not our	**pray**er before the LORD our God, that we might turn from our
Jonah 2:7	the LORD: and my	**pray**er came in unto thee, into thine holy temple.

by Dr. Ralph Stowe

From Your Lips To God's Ear

Verse	Text leading 'pray'	Text following 'pray'
2 Chr 30:27	their voice was heard, and their	prayer came up to his holy dwelling place, even unto heaven.
Ps 88:2	Let my	prayer come before thee: incline thine ear unto my cry;
Isa 56:7	shall be called an house of	prayer for all people.
2 Kings 19:4	heard: wherefore lift up thy	prayer for the remnant that are left.
Isa 37:4	heard: wherefore lift up thy	prayer for the remnant that is left.
Jer 7:16	people, neither lift up cry nor	prayer for them, neither make intercession to me: for I will not hear
2 Cor 1:11	Ye also helping together by	prayer for us, that for the gift bestowed upon us by the
2 Cor 9:14	And by their	prayer for you, which long after you for the exceeding grace of God in
Acts 10:31	And said, Cornelius, thy	prayer is heard, and thine alms are had in remembrance in the sight of
Luke 1:13	him, Fear not, Zacharias: for thy	prayer is heard; and thy wife Elisabeth shall bear thee a son, and
Job 16:17	injustice in mine hands: also my	prayer is pure.
Ps 69:13	But as for me, my	prayer is unto thee, O LORD, in an acceptable time: O God, in the
James 5:16	be healed. The effectual fervent	prayer of a righteous man availeth much.

by Dr. Ralph Stowe

From Your Lips To God's Ear

Verse	Text leading 'pray'	Text following 'pray'
James 5:15	And the	**pray**er of faith shall save the sick, and the Lord shall raise him up; and
Hab 3:1	A	**pray**er of Habakkuk the prophet upon Shigionoth.
Phil 1:4	Always in every	**pray**er of mine for you all making request with joy,
Ps 102:17	He will regard the	**pray**er of the destitute, and not despise their **pray**er.
Prov 15:29	the wicked: but he heareth the	**pray**er of the righteous.
Prov 15:8	to the LORD: but the	**pray**er of the upright is his delight.
Ps 80:4	wilt thou be angry against the	**pray**er of thy people?
Dan 9:17	therefore, O our God, hear the	**pray**er of thy servant, and his supplications, and cause thy face to
2 Chr 6:19	Have respect therefore to the	**pray**er of thy servant, and to his
Neh 1:11	thine ear be attentive to the	**pray**er of thy servant, and to the **pray**er of thy servants,
Neh 1:6	, that thou mayest hear the	**pray**er of thy servant, which I **pray** before thee now, day
Neh 1:11	of thy servant, and to the	**pray**er of thy servants, who desire to fear thy name: and
2 Chr 6:29	Then what	**pray**er or what supplication soever shall be made of any man, or of all
Ps 88:13	; and in the morning shall my	**pray**er prevent thee.

by Dr. Ralph Stowe   231

From Your Lips To God's Ear

Verse	Text leading 'pray'	Text following 'pray'
Ps 35:13	my soul with fasting; and my	**pray**er returned into mine own bosom.
Prov 28:9	from hearing the law, even his	**pray**er shall be abomination.
Lam 3:44	thyself with a cloud, that our	**pray**er should not pass through.
2 Chr 6:40	let thine ears be attent unto the	**pray**er that is made in this place.
2 Chr 7:15	and mine ears attent unto the	**pray**er that is made in this place.
Rom 10:1	Brethren, my heart's desire and	**pray**er to God for Israel is, that they might be saved.
Luke 6:12	**pray**, and continued all night in	**pray**er to God.
Job 22:27	Thou shalt make thy	**pray**er unto him, and he shall hear thee, and thou shalt pay thy vows.
2 Chr 33:18	of the acts of Manasseh, and his	**pray**er unto his God, and the words of the seers that spake to him in the
Neh 4:9	Nevertheless we made our	**pray**er unto our God, and set a watch against them day and night,
Ps 42:8	song shall be with me, and my	**pray**er unto the God of my life.
Ps 5:3	in the morning will I direct my	**pray**er unto thee, and will look up.
2 Sam 7:27	found in his heart to **pray** this	**pray**er unto thee.
Acts 12:5	was kept in prison: but	**pray**er was made without ceasing of the church unto God for him.

by Dr. Ralph Stowe

From Your Lips To God's Ear

Verse	Text leading 'pray'	Text following 'pray'
Acts 16:13	of the city by a river side, where	**pray**er was wont to be made; and we sat down, and spake unto the
Isa 26:16	visited thee, they poured out a	**pray**er when thy chastening was upon them.
2 Chr 6:19	hearken unto the cry and the	**pray**er which thy servant **pray**eth before thee:
2 Chr 6:20	there; to hearken unto the	**pray**er which thy servant **pray**eth toward this place.
1 Kings 8:29	thou mayest hearken unto the	**pray**er which thy servant shall make toward this place.
Acts 16:16	it came to pass, as we went to	**pray**er, a certain damsel possessed with a spirit of divination met us,
2 Chr 7:12	said unto him, I have heard thy	**pray**er, and have chosen this place to myself for an house of sacrifice.
Phil 1:19	to my salvation through your	**pray**er, and the supply of the Spirit of Jesus Christ,
Acts 6:4	will give ourselves continually to	**pray**er, and to the ministry of the word.
Luke 22:45	And when he rose up from	**pray**er, and was come to his disciples, he found them sleeping for
Col 4:2	Continue in	**pray**er, and watch in the same with thanksgiving;
Acts 3:1	into the temple at the hour of	**pray**er, being the ninth hour.
Matt 21:22	, whatsoever ye shall ask in	**pray**er, believing, ye shall receive.
Dan 9:21	Yea, whiles I was speaking in	**pray**er, even the man Gabriel, whom I had seen in the vision at the

by Dr. Ralph Stowe

From Your Lips To God's Ear

Verse	Text leading 'pray'	Text following 'pray'
Isa 38:5	thy father, I have heard thy	**pray**er, I have seen thy tears: behold, I will add unto thy days
2 Kings 20:5	thy father, I have heard thy	**pray**er, I have seen thy tears: behold, I will heal thee: on the third
Ps 66:20	which hath not turned away my	**pray**er, nor his mercy from me.
Ps 55:1	Give ear to my	**pray**er, O God; and hide not thyself from my supplication.
Ps 54:2	Hear my	**pray**er, O God; give ear to the words of my mouth.
Ps 39:12	Hear my	**pray**er, O LORD, and give ear unto my cry; hold not thy
Ps 102:1	Hear my	**pray**er, O LORD, and let my cry come unto thee.
Ps 143:1	Hear my	**pray**er, O LORD, give ear to my supplications: in thy
Ps 17:1	unto my cry, give ear unto my	**pray**er, that goeth not out of feigned lips.
Ps 65:2	O thou that hearest	**pray**er, unto thee shall all flesh come.
1 Kings 8:28	unto the cry and to the	**pray**er, which thy servant **pray**eth before thee to day:
1 Pet 4:7	therefore sober, and watch unto	**pray**er.
1 Tim 4:5	by the word of God and	**pray**er.
Lam 3:8	and shout, he shutteth out my	**pray**er.
Ps 4:1	mercy upon me, and hear my	**pray**er.

by Dr. Ralph Stowe

From Your Lips To God's Ear

Verse	Text leading 'pray'	Text following 'pray'
Ps 6:9	; the LORD will receive my	**pray**er.
Ps 61:1	my cry, O God; attend unto my	**pray**er.
Ps 66:19	attended to the voice of my	**pray**er.
Ps 102:17	destitute, and not despise their	**pray**er.
Ps 109:4	: but I give myself unto	**pray**er.
Neh 11:17	to begin the thanksgiving in	**pray**er: and Bakbukiah the second among his brethren,
Luke 19:46	, My house is the house of	**pray**er: but ye have made it a den of thieves.
Ps 84:8	O LORD God of hosts, hear my	**pray**er: give ear, O God of Jacob. Selah.
Ps 64:1	Hear my voice, O God, in my	**pray**er: preserve my life from fear of the enemy.
Isa 56:7	them joyful in my house of	**pray**er: their burnt offerings and their sacrifices shall be
Matt 23:14	, and for a pretence make long	**pray**er: therefore ye shall receive the greater damnation.
Rom 12:12	tribulation; continuing instant in	**pray**er;
Ps 86:6	Give ear, O LORD, unto my	**pray**er; and attend to the voice of my supplications.
1 Cor 7:5	give yourselves to fasting and	**pray**er; and come together again, that Satan tempt you not for your
Matt 21:13	shall be called the house of	**pray**er; but ye have made it a den of thieves.

by Dr. Ralph Stowe   235

From Your Lips To God's Ear

Verse	Text leading 'pray'	Text following 'pray'
Mark 11:17	called of all nations the house of	**pray**er? but ye have made it a den of thieves.
Matt 6:6	But thou, when thou	**pray**est, enter into thy closet, and when thou hast shut thy
Matt 6:5	And when thou	**pray**est, thou shalt not be as the hypocrites are: for they
1 Kings 8:28	the **pray**er, which thy servant	**pray**eth before thee to day:
2 Chr 6:19	the **pray**er which thy servant	**pray**eth before thee:
2 Chr 6:20	the **pray**er which thy servant	**pray**eth toward this place.
1 Cor 14:14	an unknown tongue, my spirit	**pray**eth, but my understanding is unfruitful.
1 Kings 8:54	Solomon had made an end of	**pray**ing all this **pray**er and supplication unto the LORD,
Col 4:3	Withal	**pray**ing also for us, that God would open unto us a door of
Col 1:3	Father of our Lord Jesus Christ,	**pray**ing always for you,
Eph 6:18		**Pray**ing always with all **pray**er and supplication in the Spirit, and
Dan 6:11	assembled, and found Daniel	**pray**ing and making supplication before his God.
1 Sam 1:12	came to pass, as she continued	**pray**ing before the LORD, that Eli marked her mouth.
1Thes 3:10	Night and day	**pray**ing exceedingly that we might see your face, and might perfect
Jude 1:20	on your most holy faith,	**pray**ing in the Holy Ghost,

From Your Lips To God's Ear

Verse	Text leading 'pray'	Text following 'pray'
1 Cor 11:4	Every man	**pray**ing or prophesying, having his head covered,
1 Sam 1:26	that stood by thee here,	**pray**ing unto the LORD.
2 Cor 8:4		**Pray**ing us with much intreaty that we would receive the gift, and take
Luke 1:10	multitude of the people were	**pray**ing without at the time of incense.
Dan 9:20	And whiles I was speaking, and	**pray**ing, and confessing my sin and the sin of my people Israel, and
Mark 11:25	And when ye stand	**pray**ing, forgive, if ye have ought against any: that your
Luke 9:18	it came to pass, as he was alone	**pray**ing, his disciples were with him: and he asked them, saying, Whom
2 Chr 7:1	Solomon had made an end of	**pray**ing, the fire came down from heaven, and consumed the burnt
Luke 3:21	Jesus also being baptized, and	**pray**ing, the heaven was opened,
Acts 12:12	many were gathered together	**pray**ing.
Acts 11:5	I was in the city of Joppa	**pray**ing: and in a trance I saw a vision, A certain vessel descend, as it

by Dr. Ralph Stowe

237

From Your Lips To God's Ear

About the Author

Dr. Ralph Shirley Stowe was born of Godly parents in Kankakee, Illinois on March 1, 1945. His achievements have taken him to various vocations and areas of study. Having published over fifty works in journals and presented papers, Dr. Stowe holds a patent and is currently a consultant helping to train companies and individuals become more effective in their efforts, whatever they may be.

Other topics include:
- An Effective Guide to ISO9001: 2000 Management Implementation
- An Effective Guide to ISO14001:1996 Environmental Management Implementation
- Exercises of the Care of Your Spine and Health
- The LAMB Diet: The Longevity And Mental Bio-regeneration Diet
- Financial Planning for the Beginner
- Homeopathic Polycrest Medicine for the Layman
- Longevity and Mental Bioregeneration Diet
- Emergency Underwater Repair Survey
- Basic X-Ray Physics and Principles of X-Ray Protection